D0897146

SLIPPER ORCHIDS
OF BORNEO

MAP OF BORNEO

SABAH

Kota Kinabalu · 2 · 1 Kundasang
Papar · 3 · 5 · 4 Telupid · Sandakan
Beaufort · Tambunan
Labuan · 6
Sipitang · 7 · 8 (Maliau Basin) · 9
BRUNEI
Labi · Meligan
11 · 10 · Long Pasia
12 · Pulau Sebatik
13
Bario (Kelabit Highlands) · 17
14
SARAWAK
EAST KALIMANTAN
26
18
15
Bau · Kuching · 21 · 20
16 · Sangkulirang
WEST KALIMANTAN
22
KALIMANTAN · 19
23
CENTRAL KALIMANTAN
27
24
SOUTH KALIMANTAN
25

Baram River

0   150
km

SABAH:
1. Mt. Tamboyukon (2579 m)
2. Mt. Kinabalu (4101 m)
3. Mt. Alab (1964 m)
4. Gunung Mongkobo (1830 m)
5. Gunung Mentapok (1581 m)
6. Mt. Trus Madi (2642 m)
7. Gunung Lumarku (c. 1900 m)
8. Gunung Lotung (1667 m)
9. Mt. Silam (883 m)

BRUNEI:
10. Gunung Pagon (1850 m)

SARAWAK:
11. Gunung Mulu (2376 m)
12. Gunung Murud (2423 m)

13. Gunung Batu Lawi (2043 m)
14. Gunung Dulit (1369 m)
15. Mt. Santubong (810 m)
16. Mt. Penrissen (1329 m)

KALIMANTAN:
17. Gunung Djempanga? (after Danser, 1928)
18. Gunung Kongkemul (Gunung Kemoel) (2020 m)
19. Bukit Lesong (Bukit Batoe Lesoeng) (1730 m)
20. Mt. Ilas Mapulu ?
21. Mt. Ilas Bungaan ?
22. Gunung Kelam (1002 m)
23. Bukit Raja (2278 m)
24. Gunung Besar (1892 m)
25. Gunung Sakoembang (950 m)
26. Apokayan Highlands
27. Meratus Mountains

SLIPPER ORCHIDS OF BORNEO

Phillip Cribb
Royal Botanic Gardens
Kew

With a Foreword by
Tan Jiew Hoe

and photographs by
G. Argent, J. Asher, T.J. Barkman,
R.S. Beaman, C.L. Chan, J.B. Comber,
J. Dransfield, E. Grell, P. Hans Hazebroek,
A. Lamb, S.P. Lim, W.M. Poon, K.M. Wong,
Yii Puan Ching, and the author

Natural History Publications
Kota Kinabalu

1997

Published by

Natural History Publications (Borneo) Sdn. Bhd.,
A913, 9th Floor, Wisma Merdeka,
P.O. Box 13908,
88846 Kota Kinabalu, Sabah, Malaysia
Tel: 088-233098 Fax: 088-240768
e-mail: chewlun@tm.net.my

First published 1997

Slipper Orchids of Borneo
   by Phillip Cribb

Frontispiece: *Paphiopedilum philippinense* in Sabah *(Photo: S.P. Lim)*.

A project made possible through the kind interest of Mr Chu Chee Kuen.

Perpustakaan Negara Malaysia Cataloguing-in-Publication Data

Cribb, Phillip
    Slipper Orchids of Borneo / Phillip Cribb; with a foreword
    by Tan Jiew Hoe; and photographs by G. Argent...[et al.].
    Bibliography: p. 108-113
    Includes index
    ISBN 983-812-018-9
    1. Slipper Orchids-Borneo. I. Tan, Jiew Hoe. II. Argent, G. III. Title.
    548.15095983

Colour separations by Far East Offset & Engraving Sdn. Bhd., Kuala Lumpur
Printed in Malaysia

"One kind of the beautiful genus Cypripedium, or Ladies' Slipper, so named for its curious form of the labellum, far surpasses in beauty any of its tribe from other countries."

Hugh Low (1848) (*in* SARAWAK. R. Bentley, London)

P.J. Cribb

Contents

Foreword   ix

    Introduction   1

    The Slipper Orchid   5

    The History of Discovery in Borneo   9

    Ecology   15

    Life History   19

    Pollination   21

    Conservation   25

    Classification   27

    The species   31

    Are there more Slipper orchids to be found in Borneo?   106

Bibliography and Further Reading   108

Acknowledgements   114

Index   115

S.P. Lim

Foreword

It is now exactly a century and a half since the first slipper orchid was discovered in Borneo. The great beauty of slipper orchids, their value in the horticultural trade, their scarcity and in some cases their rarity, make them a truly special group of plants.

It is timely that Dr Phillip Cribb, the slipper orchid specialist, has produced this book. By his examination of twelve species of these fascinating plants, beautifully illustrated, he has extended our knowledge of these plants and raised our awareness that in the wild they and many other species have reached crisis stage. This is due to many factors, among them reckless and indiscriminate collection.

Dr Cribb's book enables us to visit these beautiful plants, enjoy them and at the same time be conscious that these and other orchid species are not for selfish enjoyment or exploitation and that we should not be indifferent to alteration to their habitat but they and others are part of the heritage of man.

Tan Jiew Hoe
Singapore

P.J. Cribb

Introduction

S lipper orchids have fascinated generations of naturalists and orchid growers because of their bizarre and often beautiful flowers. The species are prized even today when far more flamboyant hybrids are freely available in commerce. This has led to many species becoming rare in nature because collecting of wild plants is still considered a valid exercise by a minority of dealers. This is particularly sad when large numbers of plants can be easily grown from seed in cultivation. The

A. Lamb

Fig. 1. *Paphiopedilum dayanum* in Sabah.

Fig. 2 (opposite). Kayan River, Kalimantan, Indonesian Borneo. The habitat of *Paphiopedilum lowii.*

1

resulting offspring often produce
flowers that are considerably
superior to those of wild-collected
material because the parental clones
are of selected forms which them-
selves have fine flowers.

Borneo is well endowed with
orchids (Wood & Cribb 1994),
having one of the richest orchid
floras in the world. Amongst these
can be found twelve species of
slipper orchid, all belonging to the
genus *Paphiopedilum*. Only China
(18 species) and Thailand (13
species) have more native species
of this fascinating genus. In this
book I hope to show something of
the fascination of slipper orchids
and enthuse readers to help protect
the remaining sites where these
plants grow.

Fig. 3. Mount Kinabalu, the focal
point of the world-renowned Kinabalu
Park, is home to the most spectacular
slipper orchid known—*Paphiopedilum
rothschildianum*—which has only been
found growing on three localised sites
on this mountain.

W.M. Poon

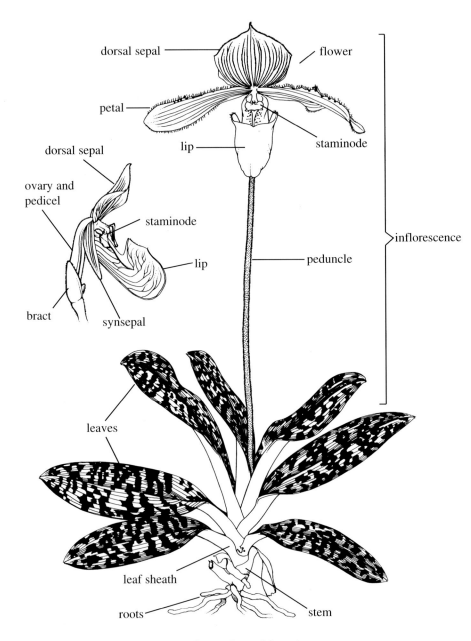

Fig. 4. Parts of a *Paphiopedilum* plant.

The Slipper Orchid

S lipper orchids are characterized by their curious flowers and gain their common name from their slipper-shaped lower petal. Another common name given to the group is Lady's Slippers, the lady being Venus. Their generic name also derives from the presence of this strange organ: Paphos refers to the place on the island of Cyprus considered in Greek mythology to be the birthplace of Aphrodite (or Venus), while 'pedilon' is the Greek for a shoe or slipper. Slipper orchids differ from other orchids in their flower structure: most notably the presence of the lip and of two, rather than one, fertile anthers.

THE PLANT

Paphiopedilum plants have very short stems bearing a number of distichously arranged (opposite and alternate) leaves. At the base of the stem several strong boot-lace like roots emerge and these are usually hairy. The roots emanate from the base of the stem, often through the leaf sheaths. The leaves are usually strap-like or obovate and spreading, especially as they age. Each is articultated to a channelled leaf sheath, the sheaths being closely overlapping and imbricate on the stem. Glossy green leaves are characteristic of the multi-flowered Bornean species, but the single-flowered species have leaves that are chequered or tessellated above with light and dark green and can have varying degrees of purple flushing beneath. Plants may have one to twenty or more growths which are usually clustered.

THE INFLORESCENCE

The Bornean species divide conveniently into those species with three or more flowers per inflorescence (rarely two flowers) and those that have a single flower. The multi-flowered species have long, suberect to spreading, hairy flower stalks (peduncles) bearing the flowers in the upper third or quarter. The bracts are usually large and boat-shaped with marginal ciliae and hairs on the central vein on the outer side. Those of *P. rothschildianum*, *P. supardii* and *P. stonei* are pale yellow with bold purple longitudinal stripes. The flowers of the multi-flowered species usually open within a few days of each other and last for several weeks. The single-flowered species have more or less erect, hairy flower stalks. The flower lasts for several weeks. The bud of a second flower can usually be found inside the bract but this usually aborts. Occasionally a second flower is borne in species that are usually single-flowered but this is a rare occurrence.

THE FLOWER

The flowers of slipper orchids are their most distinctive feature. As in all orchids the ovary is inferior, i.e. borne below the sepals and other floral segments. In most Bornean species the ovary is hairy but in *P. rothschildianum*, *P. stonei*, *P. kolopakingii* and *P. supardii* it is glabrous. The flowers have two sepals, the upper one, called the dorsal sepal, is large and usually boldly marked with stripes on a plane background. It lies opposite and above the lip, possibly sheltering the lip opening from rain. The lower sepal is called the synsepal because it is formed from the fusion of the two lower lateral sepals. Its origin is sometimes apparent because of its venation pattern and its split tip.

The petals of a slipper orchid can be readily distinguished. The two lateral petals are found each side of the dorsal sepal and usually are spreading slightly below the horizontal. In most multi-flowered species

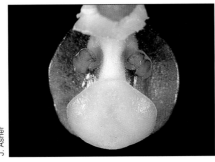

J. Asher

Fig. 5 (above). Column from below showing stigma, staminode and lateral anthers.

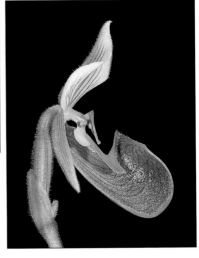

J. Asher

Fig. 6 (right). A longitudinal section of a typical *Paphiopedilum* flower.

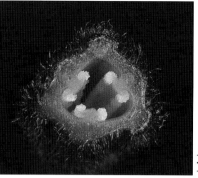

J. Asher

J. Asher

Fig. 7 (left). Column, side view. **Fig. 8** (right). Cross section of ovary.

the petals are elongate, taper to the apex and are more or less spiral. These features are particularly marked in *P. sanderianum* where the petals hang and reach a metre or more long. In *P. lowii* and the single-flowered species the petals are more or less spatulate. marginal ciliae are common and all species have petals with hairs towards the base. All of the multi-flowered species, except *P. lowii*, have glandular tips to the petals.

The third petal of slipper orchids is highly modified into a slipper-shaped lip which forms a trap for potential pollinating insects. the side lobes of the lip are incurved but are much reduced in width in the multi-flowered species allied to *P. rothschildianum*. In the single-flowered species the side lobes may be warty and glossy. The midlobe is slipper-shaped and deeply urceolate. It may be shortly pubescent on the outer surface but is usually glossy. Within, a ladder of hairs runs up the centre providing a 'ladder' up which insects can crawl to escape from the lip. The escape route takes the insects below the column with an exit either side of the base of the column behind the anthers.

The male and female organs of the orchid are united into a stalk-like column in the centre of the flower. The main feature of the column is a prominent apical shield-like staminode (sterile stamen). The shape, colour and hairiness of the staminode are important features when trying to identify the species. Behind and below the staminode lies a stalked stigma, usually with a papillose suface. Two anthers lie behind the stigma and on the sides of the column stalk. Each contains its pollen in a sticky mass.

Fig. 9. John Lindley (1799–1865), is considered the "father" of orchid taxonomy. He was Assistant Secretary of the Horticultural Society of London and eventually its Secretary.

The History of Slipper Orchid Discovery in Borneo

Hugh Low (later Sir Hugh Low, page v), Rajah Brooke's colonial treasurer for Sarawak, discovered the first slipper orchid in Borneo in 1846 on the first ascent of Mount Kinabalu by a European. It was named in his honour by John Lindley (Fig. 9). The quotation at the beginning of this book indicates the excitement Low felt about his discovery. *Paphiopedilum lowii* is indeed a fine orchid but some of the later discoveries far outshine it for beauty. Low discovered five other Bornean slipper orchids, *P. dayanum* (1856), *P. stonei* (1862), *P. javanicum* var. *virens* (1862), *P. hookerae* (1863) and *P. bullenianum* (1865). The most exciting of these was undoubtedly *P. stonei*, a multi-flowered species, which can still be found growing close to Kuching, the capital of Sarawak. Low's finest discovery was *P. stonei* var. *platytaenium*, a variant with petals over a centimetre broad, which proved to be one of the most sought after of all orchids. It is now known to be a chance mutation and subsequent efforts by other collectors to find more plants proved abortive. Low also discovered *P. dayanum* which is one of the rarest of all species and endemic to a small area on Mount Kinabalu. Surprisingly, Low missed the spectacular *P. rothschildianum* which grows with *P. dayanum* in some localities. In common with *P. hookerae*, another of his discoveries, *P. dayanum* has beautifully tessellated leaves, unlike many other orchids, making it a desirable plant whether in flower or not. Low sent his plants back to the family nursery of Messrs. Hugh Low of Clapton, one of the pioneering orchid nurseries of Victorian England.

The lure of spectacular novelties tempted other nurseries to join in the search for orchids and other plants in Borneo. Messrs. James Veitch & Sons of Exeter and Chelsea sent Frederick Burbidge (Fig. 11) there. He did not disappoint them when he sent back in 1878 *P. lawrenceanum*, a slipper orchid which has the finest foliage of all the tessellated species and is the parent of the popular hybrid *Paphiopedilum* Maudiae, one of the most widely grown of all orchids. Frederick Sander (Fig. 10), the self-proclaimed 'Orchid King' of Sander & Sons of St. Albans, sent J. Förstermann to Borneo and was rewarded by the discovery of the strangest of all slipper orchids, the bizarre *P. sanderianum* which has pendent petals that reach a metre or more in length. This orchid survived in cultivation until the turn of the century from Förstermann's introduction but then disappeared. It remained an enigma until the late 1970s when it was rediscovered on a survey of the limestone region of Gunung Mulu in northern Sarawak by the Royal Geographical Society.

The discovery of *Paphiopedilum rothschildianum*, which many people consider to be the finest of all wild orchids, was made in 1885 by one of the orchid collectors sent to the Far East by the Belgian nursery of Jean Linden. It was again collected on 19th February 1886 by John Whitehead, a British zoologist surveying the fauna of Mount Kinabalu. In his account he describes finding "a very fine *Cypripedium* … growing amongst the piles of loose rock on top of the hills. This species, of which I made a sketch, I am told is *C. rothschildianum*, the same species as is found in New Guinea: this seems to me too improbable". He was correct, this misleading information probably being given him by Sander to whom he sent plants.

The discovery of *P. sanderianum* and *P. rothschildianum* led to a positive 'feeding frenzy' amongst the European orchid nurseries who each sent out collectors to scour the island for these and other novelties. An idea of the scale of collecting can be gauged in the letters of the collector Ericsson to Frederick Sander between April 1887 and November 1894. Just a few of these will suffice: Ericsson sent 4500 slipper orchids to Sander from Sarawak on 4th April 1887. He collected *P. rothschildianum* in September 1888, noting that 'where Cyp. Sand. grows a boat can go strait [*sic*] to the mountains a very easy thing, where the Cyp. Rot. grow the plants must be carried over the mountains over the river for about 4 days'. Nevertheless he sent 4000 plants of the latter to Sander in December, noting that Ravensway's collector was also gathering them. Despite writing in October 1888 "I think after this trip we give up Borneo altogether for here everybody is collecting Orchis a perfect

10

Fig. 10. H. Frederick Sander (1847–1920), the self-styled "Orchid King", ran large nurseries at St. Albans and in Belgium. He sent out many orchid collectors in the latter part of the last century.

Fig. 11. Frederick Burbidge (1847–1905), collected orchids and pitcher plants in Borneo for the nursery of James Veitch and Sons of Chelsea, London. He is the author of *The Gardens of the Sun*.

11

Fig. 12. Heinrich G. Reichenbach (1824–1889), took over on Lindley's death the mantle of the leading authority on orchid taxonomy.

Fig. 13. John Day (1824–1888), a well-known amateur orchid grower who painted orchids in his and other large collections in London over a period of nearly 30 years. His original watercolour paintings are at Kew.

nuisance" he continued to send more orchids: another 120 plants in November 1889, together with 1300 plants of *P. sanderianum*. In July 1890 he sent 6 cases each of *P. hookerae* and *P. rothschildianum*; more collected by Dumas in April 1893, and 3000 collected by Waterstradt in May 1895. *P. lawrenceanum* suffered similar depredation with a consignment being sent in June 1888, 1500 in May 1889 and another consignment in November 1894.

Nearly a century passed before further novelties were discovered in Borneo. The first of these was found by Ed de Vogel (Fig. 14) of Leiden University who was collecting in the Meratus Mountains of Southeast Kalimantan. He photographed and pressed a strange slipper orchid specimen growing on limestone. It remained undescribed until 1985 when plants, discovered by Supardi who was collecting for the Simanis Nursery in East Java, flowered in cultivation and were described as *P. supardii*. It has flowers that are similar to those of *P. rothchildianum* but

Fig. 14. William Boxall (1844–1910), collected orchids in Borneo and elsewhere in the Far East for the nursery of James Veitch and Sons of Chelsea, London.

K.M. Wong

Fig. 15. Ed de Vogel of the Rijksherbarium of Leiden University who discovered *Paphiopedilum supardii* in Kalimantan, Indonesian Borneo in 1972.

they lack the magnificent spreading petals of that species, the petals of *P. supardii* being twisted to give somewhat distorted appearance to the flower. In 1982 the same nursery also introduced the multi-flowered *P. kolopakingii*, named after the owner of the nursery. It has inflorescences with more flowers than any other Bornean species but they lack the magnificence of *P. rothschildianum, P. sanderianum* and *P. stonei*.

The rediscovery of *P. sanderianum* in the 1978 unfortunately sparked of a resurgence of interest in Bornean slipper orchids amongst growers, leading to a return of the commercial orchid collector to the island. Several species have been overcollected and illegally exported as a result. Sadly some of these were taken from protected areas. The most recent discovery of a slipper orchid in Borneo is that of *P. philippinense*, found growing on limestone on an island off the east coast of Sabah in 1983. This species is widespread in the Philippines, being particularly common on the long thin island of Palawan which lies to the north-east of Borneo.

It would be foolish to suggest that we know all of the slipper orchids that grow in Borneo. New species may yet lie undiscovered in the interior of the island. The rapid rate of deforestation may, however, means that the days when novelties can be found are limited.

Ecology

S lipper orchids can be found in three situations in Borneo: on the ground, growing terrestrially; on trees as epiphytes; and on rocks as lithophytes. Five species, *P. bullenianum, P. dayanum, P. javanicum, P. hookerae* and *P. lawrenceanum*, are truly terrestrial, growing in shallow leaf litter and well-drained soil on ridges and steep slopes. Only one species, the widespread *P. lowii*, is epiphytic. It grows in large trees on the larger branches and in the crotches near the main trunk. I have seen it growing in quantity on trees overhanging a river in central Borneo, one tree having 60 large plants on it. The remaining six species are lithophytic, or very rarely terrestrial or epiphytic. In the most extreme cases of *P. sanderianum, P. philippinense, P. supardii* and *P. stonei*, the roots are strongly attached to the rock substrate allowing the plants to grow on almost vertical cliffs and ledges. The other two species, *P. rothschildianum* and *P. kolopakingii*, grow on ledges on steep slopes and cliffs.

Slipper orchids can be found on a variety of substrates, all nutrient-poor. *P. bullenianum* grows in Sarawak in peat-swamp forest at the bases of small trees on slight peat hummocks. The conditions here must be acidic. In contrast *P. stonei, P. supardii, P. sanderianum* and *P. philippinense* grow on limestone rock where the pH is either alkaline or more often more or less neutral. *P. rothschildianum, P. hookerae* var. *volonteanum* and *P. dayanum* grow on ultramafic rocks that have a very peculiar flora on which the dominant tree is *Gymnostoma sumatrana*. The exact habitat preferences of *P. kolopakingii* and *P. lawrenceanum* remain a mystery.

The terrestrial species with tessellated leaves grow in deep shade on the forest floor, whereas the plain-leaved species grow in dappled shade of open woodland, often on cliffs and just below ridge-tops. North and north-east facing slopes are preferred by some species such as *P.*

Fig. 16. The Lohan River valley on the lower slopes of Mount Kinabalu, a former habitat of *Paphiopedilum rothschildianum.*

Fig. 17. Hills near the beach in southern Sarawak, the haunt of *Paphiopedilum bullenianum.*

Fig. 18. A limestone hill in southeast Sarawak, the habitat of *Paphiopedilum stonei*.

sanderianum, *P. stonei* and *P. rothschildianum*, but the preferences of most species remain unknown. Moisture levels around the roots, soil type and pH,, availability of mycorrhizal fungi and suitable pollinators, and light levels are all critical factors in the establishment and success of *Paphiopedilum* colonies.

Paphiopedilums grow in small colonies, rarely extending more than 100 m across and 50 m in elevation. Colonies I have seen range from 100 plants or less *in P. dayanum, P. sanderianum* and *P. stonei* to many hundreds in *P. javanicum* and *P. rothschildianum*. However, since most Bornean species are very restricted in distribution, often being endemic to one mountain or range, even the numerically strong species are very localised. Only *P. lowii* and *P. bullenianum* are at all widespread in the island and both, together with *P. philippinense*, are also found elsewhere in the Malay Archipelago.

Life History

S lipper orchids have small seeds weighing about 1 to 2 mg and range from 0.11 to 1.97 mm long and 0.07 to 0.4 mm across. They are fusiform in shape and undoubtedly wind-dispersed. The embryo consists of a few dozen cells and is surrounded by a relatively impermeable coat of cells derived from the ovule's inner integument and testa of dead cells derived from the outer integument. Orchid seeds do not have any endosperm and rely for nutrition upon an intimate association with a mycorrhizal fungus.

The seeds mature between nine and twelve months after fertilization and disperse through slits in the capsule that develop as it turns brown and dries out. Germination for most species probably occurs soon after dispersal. Germination occurs in the dark in the soil or on a suitable substrate. The protocorm produces long rhizoids which become infected with mycorrhizal hyphae. A root soon emerges behind the shoot apex. The rhizomatous protocorm elongates and produces further roots. The first leaf appears a few months after germination. The first root, which contains little xylem but copious phloem, is covered in rhizoids and is mycotrophic from the start. The cortex is densely infected with fungal pelotons. However, later roots are progressively less infected and by the fifth, the roots are characteristically slender with well-developed xylem and a lack of pelotons.

In mature plants the bud containing the leaves and inflorescence for the following year develops during the previous growing season. The new growth begins to develop even before flowering has finished.

Flowering occurs at the end of the rains in most Bornean slipper orchids. February to April is the best season to see slipper orchids in flower but flowering can also occur in November. Flowers last for between four to eight weeks.

Slipper orchids can live for many years. Hybrid slipper orchids that were made by growers in Europe in the last two decades of the 19th century are still going strong after more than a century in cultivation. It seems unlikely that plants would survive as long in the wild because their habitats will change over the years and become progressively less suitable for their survival. Nevertheless, plants of some species with up to twenty mature growths can be found, suggesting that they have survived for a number of years.

Pollination

T he distinctive flowers of slipper orchids are marked by the inflated slipper or shoe-shaped lip which lies ventrally in the open flower. The lip has a large opening on its upper surface enclosed by the incurved margins of the lip. The staminode blocks the opening at the base of the lip leaving just two small openings or orifices, one on each side of the column at its base. The inside of the lip is covered in hairs, particularly in the basal part. On the column the staminode is the most prominent organ in most species. The stalked stigma lies behind it on the ventral side of the column and an anther lies just behind the stigma on each side. Based on his knowledge of the flower, Charles Darwin (1862), in his hugely influential account of orchid pollination, suggested that pollination of the European *Cypripedium calceolus* was effected by an insect sitting on the outside of the lip and reaching the pollen by inserting its mouthparts through the basal orifices of the lip.

Subsequently, this has been shown to be erroneous. Visiting insects, notably bees and hover flies, enter the lip, attracted by flower colour, floral fragrance which is rich in acetates that appear to mimic pheromone secretions of some bees and flies, and also by the colour patterns of the staminode and lip which are false nectar guides. It has been suggested that the fragrance chemicals might upset the landing control pheromones of bees alighting on the lip thereby increasing the likelihood of them slipping into the pouched lip.

Once inside the lip the insects seldom escape by the route through which they entered. Rather, they exit if at all out of the base of the lip through the basal orifices. The expanded stigma acts as the essential support to allow pollinators to bend down the lip and thence pass under the anthers and out through the basal orifices. Only insects of the right size, neither too large nor too small, can pass out of the lip this way to effect pollination.

The lips of many slipper orchids have areas of unpigmented tissue, so called "windows", in the lateral part of the posterior region of the lip. These have been suggested as inducing phototaxis in pollinators to lead them out the correct way (Webster, 1886; Troll, 1951). However, the evidence for this is inconclusive (Nilsson, 1979).

Dodson & van der Pijl (1966) in their excellent account of the pollination and evolution of orchid flowers suggested that *Paphiopedilum* and *Phragmipedium* have trap flowers that are, at least in part, fly-pollinated whereas *Cypripedium* and possibly *Selenipedium* flowers are bee-pollinated.

The lurid floral coloration and the 'curious furry warts' and spots on the floral segments of some species are cited by Dodson & van der Pijl (1966) and by Atwood (1985) as typical of adaptations in flowers that attract flies. The long tail-like petals of *P. sanderianum*, for example, might serve the same function.

Cross-pollination by insects is certainly prevalent in *Paphiopedilum*. Self-pollination is not known in *Paphiopedilum*. Delpino (1873) mentioned an "odore spermatico-urinoso" in *P. villosum* and *P. purpuratum* and suggested fly-pollination for the group corroborated by his finding bluebottles trapped in the lip of *P. barbatum* in a greenhouse in Italy. Schlechter (1927) made similar observations while Ziegenspeck (1928) found the same in *P. insigne*. Atwood (1985) has observed syrphid flies in the lip of *P. hennisianum* in cultivation in Florida, and I have seen them in the lips of *P. lowii* in the wild and *P. philippinense* in cultivation in the Far East.

The only detailed study in the field of pollination of *Paphiopedilum* in Borneo is that of Atwood (1985) who studied *P. rothschildianum* on Mount Kinabalu. The syrphid fly, *Dideopsis aegrota*, was found to be its pollinator. The flowers, emitting a 'peppery or spicy fragrance', are considered to mimic brood sites to attract gravid female flies to the staminode where they lay their eggs. Atwood found as many as 76 eggs on a single staminode. After alighting on the staminode, which has a glabrous front, the fly falls into the lip and can only escape by crawling up the hairs, which lead it beneath the stigma and anthers in turn, to emerge eventually from one of two exits on either side of the base of the

Fig. 19. Close-up of the staminode of *Paphiopedilum rothschildianum.*

C.L. Chan

column. Pollination is affected when the fly repeats the manoeuvre in a second flower. The fly apparently gains no benefit from its experience as the eggs either do not hatch or else the larvae die on hatching from lack of food. Likewise, the fly receives no food benefit from its visit as the flower lacks nectar. Atwood suggests that the glandular hairs on the staminode mimic a colony of aphids, the normal brood site of the fly.

Atwood also studied colonies of *P. hookerae* var. *volonteanum* and *P. javanicum* var. *virens* which also grow on Mount Kinabalu but was unable to determine the pollinators. From 18 observed flowers of the latter he noted that three had been pollinated in a six week period after anthesis. The high seed production in successful pollinations no doubt explains this low success rate. A single syrphid egg was found on the staminode of *P. hookerae* var. *volonteanum* but as it was growing near *P. rothschildianum* little could be concluded from the observation.

In 1983, on a visit to Kinabalu, I collected a dead syrphid fly trapped between the base of the lip and column of *P. javanicum* var. *virens*. I have yet to identify the fly but the fact that it had been trapped and had died suggests that a smaller species might be the normal pollinator

Atwood's study gives no clue as to the function of the long petals of *P. rothschildianum* and his work suggests that the floral fragrance eminates from the centre of the flower rather than from the glandular petal tips as noted in *Phragmipedium* by Vogel (1962). The enigma of the metre-long petals of *P. sanderianum* remains to tantalise pollination biologists.

A recent study of the pollination of *P. villosum* in Thailand by Bänziger (1996) has also suggested that hover-flies are its main pollinators.

P.J. Cribb

Fig. 20. Hoverfly eggs are seen on the stamminode of *Paphiopedilum philippinense*.

Conservation

All of the Bornean slipper orchids are rare, their colonies usually being small and widely separated. This has made them vulnerable to habitat change and destruction, and also to collection for the horticultural trade. Currently the deforestation of large tracts of lowland and lower montane forest in Borneo is probably the greatest long-term threat to these plants. In particular, the recurrent cycle of drought and forest fires brought on by 'El Niño' has destroyed large tracts of lowland and hill forest, including some localities where slipper orchids previously thrived.

The threat from collecting for trade remains a problem, particularly for the high-profile species such as *P. sanderianum* and *P. rothschildianum*. Protection of some of the best populations within National Parks and Forest Reserves cannot entirely remove the threat posed by collectors. Of the twelve species in Borneo, five receive protection in the Kinabalu Park in Sabah, two in the Gunung Mulu National Park, and one in the Bako National Park in Sarawak. The international trade in wild-collected species slipper orchids has been somewhat curtailed by the placing of all *Paphiopedilum* species on Appendix I of CITES (Convention in Trade on Endangered Species of Fauna and Fauna) in 1988. Nevertheless, some collecting still occurs both for export and for a growing internal trade in both Malaysia and Indonesia. This is a shame because selected clones of all slipper orchid species have been raised from seed and the seedlings usually have far better flowers than those of plants taken from the wild. Furthermore, the nursery-raised plants grow better and faster than the wild-collected ones.

How rare are the Bornean slipper orchids? I estimate from my own observations and from those of people who have studied them in the wild in the island that of the 12 species, *P. rothschildianum*, *P. sanderianum*, *P. stonei*, *P. supardii*, *P. kolopakingii*, *P. dayanum* and *P. lawrenceanum* must be considered to be particularly vulnerable. All are narrowly endemic to a single mountain or mountain range and have small populations that are now widely disjunct. For example, *P. rothschildianum* has only ever been found in three localities, one of which is now destroyed by fire. *P. dayanum* is known from two localities in one of which it had been reduced to less than 30 plants in 1983. Collectors could easily remove all the mature plants of most populations I have seen in a day's work. If they return within two years they can then remove the seedlings that were missed but have subsequently grown to maturity. Without the seedling buffer, the population will perish. This had happened by 1990 to the population of *P. javanicum* var. *virens* found near to the Kinabalu Park Headquarters. Commonsense suggests that if you wish to cultivate these plants buy seedlings from nurseries. If you see plants in the wild, photograph them but do not collect them.

Classification

S lipper orchids are a remarkable group within the family *Orchidaceae*. They comprise five genera: *Selenipedium*, *Phragmipedium* and *Mexipedium*, all three tropical American; *Cypripedium* with a north temperate distribution in both the Old and New Worlds; and *Paphiopedilum* found only in tropical Asia and the adjacent islands from Sumatra across to the Philippines and Solomon Islands. Altogether there are less than 150 species of slipper orchid and about half of these belong in *Paphiopedilum*, 47 in *Cypripedium*, about 12 in *Phragmipedium*, six in *Selenipedium* with a single *Mexipedium* making up the numbers.

Paphiopedilum is readily distinguished from the the genera *Cypripedium* and *Selenipedium* by its conduplicate coriaceous, rather than plicate, leaves and persistent perianth. The other conduplicate-leaved genera *Phragmipedium* and *Mexipedium* are both confined to the American tropics. *Paphiopedilum* differs from *Phragmipedium* and *Mexipedium* in having imbricate sepal vernation and a different chromosome base number; from the former it also differs in having a unilocular ovary. A detailed discussion of the generic concepts is provided by Albert (1994) and Albert & Chase (1992).

Detailed analysis of *Paphiopedilum* species using both morphological and molecular characters have elucidated the probably evolutionary relationships of the species. The Chinese and Vietnamese species of subgenus *Parvisepalum,* including *P. delenatii* and *P. micranthum*, are considered to be the most primitive. They mostly have leaves which are chequered on the upper side with light and dark green and purple-spotted beneath, and a single brightly coloured flower. The flowers suggest that they are bee-pollinated like their similarly coloured cousins in the genus *Cypripedium*. The Bornean species belong to three groups which are among the more advanced species in an evolutionary sense. The multi-flowered species of sects. *Coryopedilum* and *Pardalopetalum*, which include seven of the Bornean species, have green leaves and inflorescences bearing three to 14 flowers. The flowers tend to be ochre, green or pale yellow and spotted or striped with purple or brown. They are mostly thought to be hover-fly pollinated. The most highly evolved group includes four Bornean species of sect. *Barbata*: *P. dayanum*, *P. lawrenceanum*, *P. hookerae* and *P. javanicum*, all characterised by chequered leaves and solitary, rather drably coloured flowers which are also probably hover-fly pollinated. Three sections: *Brachypetalum*, *Paphiopedilum* and *Cochlopetalum* are not represented on the island.

KEY TO THE SPECIES

1. Plants usually with three or more flowers; leaves plain green, strap-like **2**
   Plants usually with a single flower; leaves elliptic to obovate or oblanceolate, tessellated on upper side with light and dark green ......
   .... **8**

2. Plant epiphytic; staminode flat, obcordate, with a basal hairy protuberence and trifid in apical notch; dorsal sepal obovate, not boldly striped; petals spathulate, somewhat half-twisted in apical half, boldly spotted in basal half, purple in apical half; lip side lobes well developed and incurved **3**
   Plant terrestrial or lithophytic; staminode convex, oblong, subcircular or linear, notched at apex; dorsal sepal ovate, usually boldly longitudinally striped; petals tapering from base to apex, often very spirally twisted; lip side lobes very reduced **4**

3. Ovary densely hairy .... **7. P. lowii var. lowii**
   Ovary lacking hairs .... **8. P. lowii var. lynniae**

4. Ovary densely hairy **5**
   Ovary lacking hairs **6**

5. Petals pendent, ribbon-like, 30–100 cm long; ovary white .... **2. P. sanderianum** Petals spreading at about 60 degrees below horizontal, 10–20 cm long; ovary purple .... **1. P. philippinense**

6. Staminode linear; petals spreading at about 30 degrees below horizontal to give flower a spread of between 18 and 32 cm .... **5. P. rothschildianum** Staminode not linear; petals pendent or held at 50 degrees or less below the horizontal; flowers less than 15 cm between the petal tips **7**

7. Petals unspotted, ochreous; lip ochre-coloured with darker veins; staminode reddish... **3. P. kolopakingii** Petals spotted; lip yellow or red-flushed; staminode yellow with yellow or red margins **8**

8. Dorsal sepal yellow with purple longitudinal veins; petals yellow with large purple spots, twisted in a contorted manner, less than twice the length of the lip; staminode with dense marginal red hairs .... **6. P. supardii** Dorsal sepal white, longitudinally lined with purple or plain; Petals spotted with purple, more than twice the length of the lip, slightly spirally twisted near apex; staminode pale yellow with yellow marginal hairs .... **4. P. stonei**

9. Petals more than 7 cm long, giving the flower a spread of 10 cm or more, unspotted, marginal ciliae long; dorsal sepal acuminate, white with green venation .... **13. P. dayanum** Petals less than 6 cm long, giving the flower a spread of 8 cm or less, spotted on lamina and/or margins; dorsal sepal acute **10**

10. Staminode subcircular, pubescent, notched at apex .... **11** Staminode transversely reniform, tri-dentate at broad apex **12**

11. Leaves green on under side; lip not inflated noticeably in apical half .... **9. P. hookerae var. hookerae** Leaves purple-flushed to varying degrees beneath; lip noticeably inflated in apical half .... **10. P. hookerae var. volonteanum**

12. Petals markedly spathulate, often half-twisted in apical half; dorsal sepal smaller than lip .... **9. P. bullenianum**
    Petals linear-subspathulate, spreading almost horizontally and untwisted; dorsal sepal larger than the lip **13**

13. Dorsal sepal as wide as long, obtuse, white with bold purple stripes; petals spotted on upper and lower margins only, deep purple .... **11. P. lawrenceanum**
    Dorsal sepal longer than wide, acute; petals spotted finely in basal half; green with a purple apex .... **14. P. javanicum var. virens**

The Species

1. PAPHIOPEDILUM PHILIPPINENSE

It was something of a surprise that *Paphiopedilum philippinense* was discovered some ten years or more ago in Sabah. Previously it had been considered endemic to the Philippines, albeit the most widespread of the many species of slipper orchids found there.

This, the most variable and widespread species of sect. *Coryopedilum*, was described by H.G. Reichenbach (Fig. 12) in 1862 but he did not cite a type and I have found no contemporary specimen in his herbarium labelled as such. The only sheet labelled *Cypripedium philippinense* in his herbarium has two cultivated collections on it dating from 1879.

I have no hesitation in including *Cypripedium laevigatum* in the synonymy of *P. philippinense*. James Bateman described it in 1865 without reference to the Reichenbach species. His description agrees well with that of *P. philippinense* and, in the absence of the type of the latter, it is impossible to say how the two differ.

Cypripedium roebelenii was described by Reichenbach in 1883 based on a collection by Roebelen, one of Sander's collectors. The longer pendent petals of *C. roebelenii* seems to be the only character of those cited in the protologue which distinguishes it consistently from *P. philippinense*. Both Veitch (1889) and Stein (1892) included it as a synonym of *P. philippinense*. Although resurrected at intervals since then, notably by Pfitzer (1903), Schoser (1971) and Asher (1980–81), I do not consider its petal attitude and length to be sufficient for its recognition at specific rank.

Plants introduced as *P. roebelenii* do seem to have consistently long pendent petals and it seems most satisfactory to recognise them at

31

Fig. 21. *Paphiopedilum philippinense* growing lithophytically in Sabah.

varietal level as var. *roebelenii*. Valmayor (1984) gives its distribution as Rizal (Antipolo) on the island of Luzon.

Paphiopedilum philippinense is most closely allied to *P. randsii* from the Philippines and *P. sanderianum* from Borneo. From the former, it can be readily distinguished by its longer tapering petals which are usually spirally twisted and by its smaller narrow lip. From the latter, it differs in its erect habit, much shorter petals, shorter dorsal sepal, smaller blunt lip and smaller staminode with a broader apical sinus.

Paphiopedilum philippinense is widely distributed throughout the Philippines from Luzon south to northern Mindanao and westwards to Palawan and islands of the east coast of Sabah. A small colony has recently been found growing on the mainland of Sabah. It is always found growing on limestone cliffs, hills and outcrops often in fairly open

32

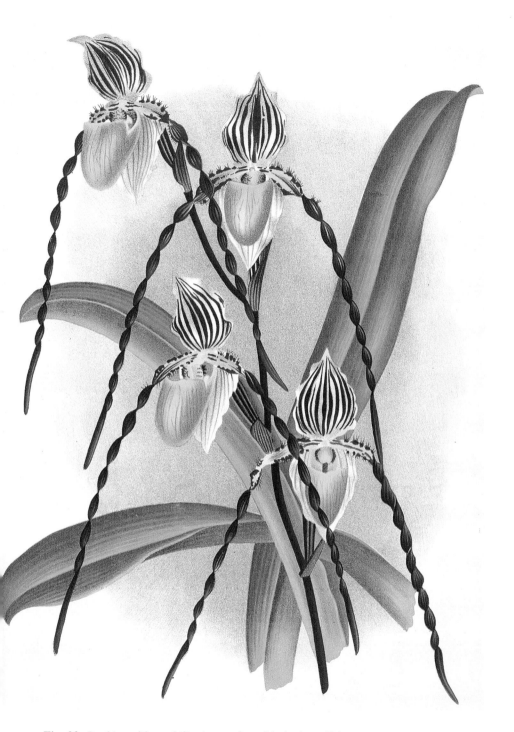

Fig. 22. *Paphiopedilum philippinense* from Lindenia t. 404.

S.P. Lim

Fig. 23. *Paphiopedilum philippinense* growing in mainland Sabah.

S.P. Lim

Fig. 24. A population of *Paphiopedilum philippinense* growing on a limestone outcrop in eastern Sabah—the first record of this species occuring on mainland Borneo.

situations in limestone rubble between 200 and 300 m above sea level. In the wild, it flowers between January and April. The Sabahan plants are referable to var. *philippinense*.

Paphiopedilum philippinense (Rchb.f.) Stein, *Orchideenbuch* 480 (1892); Pfitzer in Engler, *Pflanzenr. Orch. Pleon.* 61 (1903). Type: without provenance (holotype W ?lost).

Cypripedium philippinense Rchb.f. in *Bonplandia* 10: 335 (1862).
C. laevigatum Bateman in *Curtis's Bot. Mag.* 91: t. 5508 (1861). Type: hort. Veitch (illustration in *Curtis's Bot. Mag.* t. 5508).
Selenipedium laevigatum (Bateman) May in *Rev. Hort.* 1885: 301 (1885).
Cypripedium cannartianum Linden in *Lindenia* 3: 93, t. 141 (1888). Types: Philippines, hort. *Cannart d'Hamale* & hort. *Wallaert* (not found).
C. roebbelinii Rchb.f. var. *cannartianum* Linden in *Lindenia* 3: 93, t. 141 (1888) in synon.
Paphiopedilum laevigatum (Bateman) Pfitzer in Engler & Prantl, *Nat. Pflanzenf.* 2, 6: 84 (1889).
P. philippinense (Rchb.f.) Stein var. *cannartianum* (Linden) Pfitzer in Engler, *Pflanzenr. Orch. Pleon.* 62 (1903).

DESCRIPTION. A *terrestrial* or *lithophytic herb*. *Leaves* coriaceous, up to 9, ligulate, rounded at asymmetric apex, 20–50 cm long, 2–5.5 cm wide. V-shaped in cross-section, very thick in texture. *Inflorescence* erect, 2–4-flowered, up to 50 cm long; peduncle purple-pubescent; bracts elliptic, acute, pubescent, up to 5 cm long, 2 cm wide. *Flowers* rather variable in size; sepals white, dorsal striped with maroon; petals white or yellow at base, maroon above with marginal dark maroon warts in basal half; lip and staminode yellow; pedicel and ovary 4.5–6.5 cm long, purple, pubescent. *Dorsal sepal* ovate, acute, 4–5 cm long, 2–2.5 cm wide. *Synsepal* similar to dorsal sepal, 4.5–5.3 cm long, 2 cm wide. *Petals* linear, tapering to apex, 6–15 cm long, 5–6 mm wide, ciliate. *Lip* small, rather ovoid in shape, 2.2–3.8 cm long, 1.4 cm wide. *Staminode* convex, rather cordate-subquadrate, emarginate, yellow, veined with green, purple-pubescent on sides. $2n = 26$.

DISTRIBUTION. The Philippines, Sabah and islands off north coast of Sabah; on limestone; sea-level to *c*. 500 m. altitude.

2. PAPHIOPEDILUM SANDERIANUM

*P*aphiopedilum sanderianum, with its long dangling petals that can reach a metre or more in length, is one of the most striking of all orchids. It was discovered in Borneo in 1885 by J. Förstermann, one of Messrs. Sander's collectors. Förstermann recognised that it was a new species, describing well its narrow leaves with distinctive margins, but did not see it in flower in the wild. Always a rarity in cultivation, it has been painted only a few times, notably by John Day in his scrapbook in 1886, when it flowered for the first time in cultivation, and again by Walter Fitch for Sander's *Reichenbachia* (1888). Line drawings also appeared in Veitch's *Manual* in 1889 and in the *Gardeners' Chronicle* in 1896. By the turn of the century, it had probably disappeared from orchid collections.

Its brief sojourn in cultivation and the few preserved herbarium collections (the type in Vienna, two at Kew and two at Harvard), led Schaffer (1974) to suggest that it was either a monstrosity or a hybrid.

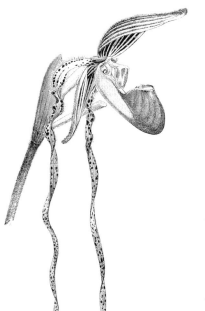

However, its rediscovery in 1978 in Sarawak by Ivan Nielsen has shown such speculation to be false (Alexander 1984).

Its extremely long pendent petals, the cause of Schaffer's suggestions, distinguish *P. sanderianum* readily from other closely allied species of sect. *Coryopedilum*. Its lip and staminode shape, and the pubescent ovary, indicate that it is most closely allied to the variable and widespread *P. philippinense*.

Paphiopedilum sanderianum grows in the wild on vertical north-east or east facing limestone cliffs from 50 to 300

Fig. 25. *P. sanderianum* from J. Veitch, *Manual of Orchidaceous Plants* IV, (1889).

Fig. 26. *Paphiopedilum sanderianum* from Reichenbachia t. 3.

Fig. 27. Flowering plants of *Paphiopedilum sanderianum* growing on a limestone cliff in Sarawak. Photographed during the Royal Geographic Society Expedition in 1978 when it was first rediscovered.

P. Hans Hazebroek

R.B.G., Kew

Fig. 29 (above). *Paphiopedilum sanderianum*, in cultivation at Kew.

A. Lamb

Fig. 30 (left). The boldly striped dorsal sepal, spirally pendent petals and forward pointing lip can be seen well in this flower of *Paphiopedilum sanderianum*.

Fig. 28 (opposite). *Paphiopedilum sanderianum*, a fine form growing in its native habitat in Sarawak.

m elevation in places that are in deep shade for most of the day, receiving diffuse sunlight only in the morning. Its roots grow in intimate contact with the surface of the rock. Its exacting habitat requirements may explain its rarity. It flowers in March and April in the wild. The reason for its extremely long petals is less clear, although it has been suggested that the petals act as an attractant for hoverflies, almotst certainly its potential pollinators, which can then climb the petals up into the pouch. Field observations are needed to test this bizarre theory. Kramer (1990) observed that a sugary solution, which he called nectar, is produced on the upper part of the outer surface of the lip and suggested that this attracts potential pollinators. However, it might also attract ants that deter predation. Field work is needed to elucidate the pollination strategy of this species.

Despite its short sojourn in cultivation at the end of the nineteenth century, *P. sanderianum* nevertheless was used as a parent in the production of eight primary and eight secondary hybrids. None of these, however, exhibited the long-petalled character of *P. sanderianum*. This has not deterred hybridists now that the species again has become available in cultivation.

Most of the colonies of this fine orchid are found within the confines of a national park. Nevertheless, it is sad to report that the closely guarded secret of the habitat of *P. sanderianum* has been discovered by commercial orchid collectors who have reportedly taken large numbers of plants from the wild for sale at high prices.

Paphiopedilum sanderianum (Rchb.f.) Stein, *Orchideenbuch* 482 (1892); Pfitzer in Engler, *Pflanzenr. Orch. Pleon.* 62 (1903); Day, *Scrapbook* 51: t. 69 (1886); Sander in *Reichenbachia* 1: 7, 7. 3 (1888); Veitch, *Man.* 2: 46 (1889); Anon. in *Gard Chron.* 19: 329, fig. 45 (1896); Schaffer in *Orchid. Dig.* 38: 233 (1974); C. Alexander in *Kew Mag.* 1(1): 3 (1984). Type: Malay Archipdago, hort. Sander (holotype W!).
Cypripedium sanderianum Rchb.f. in *Gard. Chron.* n.s. 25: 554 (1886).

DESCRIPTION. A *lithophytic herb* of one or two growths. *Leaves* 4–5, arcuate-pendent, linear, obliquely roundly or obtusely bilobed at apex, up to 45 cm long, 2.5–5.3 cm wide, shiny, green, apical leaf reduced to

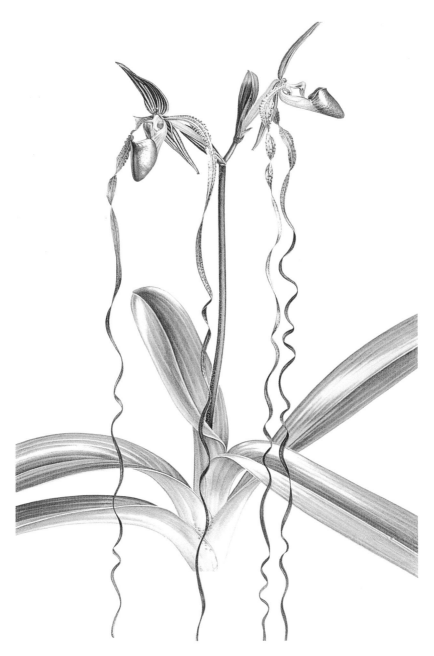

Fig. 31. *Paphiopedilum sanderianum.* (Painting by Pandora Sellars).

A. Lamb

Fig. 32. Side view of *Paphiopedilum sanderianum* showing its very pale-coloured pedicel and ovary.

a sterile bract at base of peduncle. *Inflorescence* horizontal or slightly ascending, 2–5-flowered; peduncle purple or red-brown, with short purple hairs, 8–14 cm long, 3–4 mm in diameter; bracts elliptic-lanceolate, obtuse, 3.3–5 cm long, 1.4–1.6 cm broad, red-brown with darker veins, ciliate on margins and mid-vein. *Flowers c.* 7 cm across, up to 100 cm long; sepals yellow striped with maroon; petals off-white to creamy yellow, spotted maroon in basal half, purple above; lip yellow flushed and veined brown; staminode yellow; pedicel and ovary 3.4–7 cm long, white or cream, purple-pubescent. *Dorsal sepal* lanceolate, acuminate, slightly concave, 4.2–6.5 cm long, 1.2–2.5 cm wide, purple-pubescent on outer surface. *Synsepal* lanceolate, acuminate, 3.4–6 cm long, 1–1.5 cm wide, two-keeled, purple-pubescent on outer surface. *Petals* ribbon-like, pendent, tapering to apex, linear-tapering, undulate and twisted, 23–100 cm long, 0.5–0.9 cm wide, with maroon warts on basal margins, ciliate in basal half, minutely glandular pubescent at apex. *Lip* subporrect, pointed at apex, 4–5 cm long, 1.3–2.5 cm wide; side-lobes incurved, very short, subacute. *Staminode* convex, oblong-trullate, emarginate or obscurely tridenticulate at apex, 10–13 mm long, 6–9 mm wide, pubescent on basal and side margins.

DISTRIBUTION. Borneo (Sarawak only); 50–300 m altitude.

3. PAPHIOPEDILUM KOLOPAKINGII

This extraordinary recent discovery from a remote area of central Borneo first flowered in cultivation in 1982 in the Simanis nursery of Liem Khe Wie (A. Kolopaking) at Lawang in east Java. I visited the nursery in March 1983 and saw over 50 large plants from a single collection. It was described the following year by Jack Fowlie who named it after Mr Kolopaking (Liem Khe Wie), the owner of Simanis Orchids.

Fig. 33. A close-up of a flower of *P. kolopakingii*.

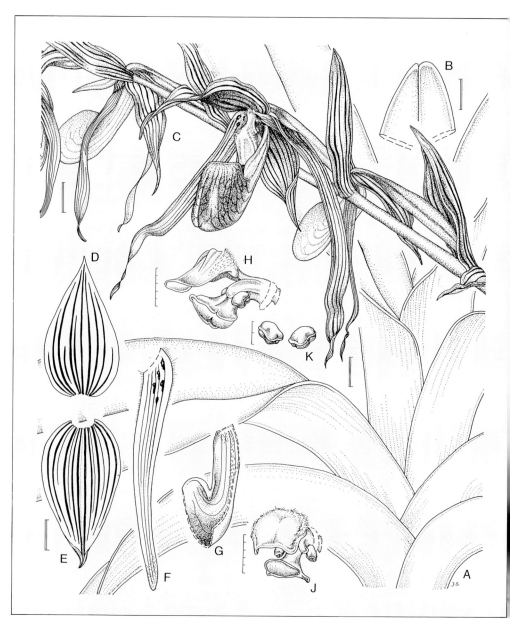

Fig. 34. *Paphiopedilum kolopakingii* Fowlie. - A: habit. - B: leaf apex. - C: part of inflorescence. - D: dorsal sepal. - E: synsepal. - F: petal.- G: lip, longitudinal section. - H: column, side view. - J: column, oblique view. - K: anthers. A–C drawn from a cultivated specimen at RBG Kew and D–K from *Fowlie* s.n. by Judi Stone. Scale: single bar divided into mm; double bar divided into cm. (Reproduced from *Orchids of Borneo Vol. 3*, page 198)

Vegetatively, the plants are not unlike those of *P. rothschildianum* but the leaves are fleshier and stand suberect to produce one of the largest plants in the genus. The flowers are not spectacular but are produced in quantity with up to 14 being counted on a single spike during the 1982 flower season by Jim Comber (pers. comm.). The flowers most closely resemble those of the allied Bornean species *P. stonei* but more are produced on each spike and they are distinctively coloured, smaller in all their parts and have a narrower staminode which is obtuse and slightly upcurved at the apex.

Paphiopedilum topperi, described by Braem and Mohr in 1988, based on a collection that flowered in the collection of Richard Topper in the U.S.A., is certainly conspecific with *P. kolopakingii* and therefore reduced here to its synonymy.

Paphiopedilum kolopakingii is still rather rare in cultivation and all plants probably originate from the Simanis nursery. However, its floriferous nature should ensure that it becomes a popular parent in hybridising. No other species produces so many flowers opening at the same time.

Hopefully, seedlings from crossing and selfings will be introduced into cultivation in some numbers in the not-too-distant future to prevent it being stripped from the wild in large quantities.

Paphiopedilum kolopakingii Fowlie in *Orchid Dig.* 48: 41 (1984). Type: Borneo, Kalimantan, hort. *Simanis Orchids* LKW 82 K1 (holotype UCLA!).
P. topperi Braem & Mohr in *Schlechteriana* 1(2): 15 (1988). Type: Kalimantan, cult. Topper (holotype SCHLE).

DESCRIPTION. A *terrestrial* or *lithophytic herb* with long fleshy roots, 5–8 mm in diameter. *Leaves* 8–10, suberect, ligulate, rounded, 40–80 cm long, 6–12 cm wide, dark green. *Inflorescence* 6–15-flowered, arcuate, 40–70 cm long; bracts elliptic-lanceolate, acuminate, 4–5 cm long, 1–1.5 cm wide, greenish-ochre, striped purple. *Flowers* 8–10 cm across; sepals whitish with dark red-brown or dark brown venation; petals green, veined with red or brown; lip olive-green to ochre with darker veins; staminode yellow; ovary and pedicel 5.5–6.5 cm long, glabrous. *Dorsal*

Fig. 35. An inflorescence of *Paphiopedilum kolopakingii* cultivated in East Java.

sepal ovate, acute to acuminate, 3.5–6.5 cm long, 2–3.5 cm wide, finely pubescent. *Synsepal* ovate-lanceolate, acute to acuminate, 3.5–5 cm long, 2–2.6 cm wide, 2-keeled on back. *Petals* deflexed, slightly spirally twisted, falcate, linear-tapering, acute, 5–7 cm long, 0.6–0.8 cm wide, finely and minutely pubescent. *Lip* rather sharp at apex, grooved behind, 4.1–6 cm long, 0.9–1.5 cm wide, with acute incurved auricles. *Staminode* convex, subquadrate, obtuse and upcurved at apex, 9–15 mm long, 5–10 mm wide, with brownish pubescent sides.

DISTRIBUTION. Borneo, central Kalimantan only; in moss on rocks near rivers, 600–1100 m altitude.

4. PAPHIOPEDILUM STONEI

The limestone cliffs and hills of western Sarawak are the home of *P. stonei*, one of the most highly prized of all species in the genus. Large importations of *P. stonei* have continued to be made since its discovery and introduction in 1862 by Messrs. Low and Co.

Sir William Hooker described it in December of that year in *Curtis's Botanical Magazine*, the forerunner of the present *Kew Magazine*, naming it for Mr Stone, the gardener of John Day of Tottenham, London. It is a striking orchid readily recognised by its boldly striped dorsal sepal, pink porrect lip, slender arcuate untwisted petals and distinctive staminode. Its closest ally is probably *P. kolopakingii*, but that has more and smaller ochreous flowers which are also less boldly marked with deep maroon.

A. Lamb

Fig. 36 (above). *Paphiopedilum stonei*. in its natural habitat in Sarawak.

Fig. 37 (left). *Paphiopedilum stonei*, a distinct form with a white dorsal sepal.

R.B.G. Kew

49

Fig. 38. *Paphiopedilum stonei* from Lindenia t. 281.

Fig. 39. *Paphiopedilum stonei* var. *platytaenium* from John Day's Scrapbook, 4th May 1878.

Despite the frequent appearance of jungle-collected plants in the trade, *P. stonei* has a very limited distribution and its frequent re-collection must inevitably have severely depleted it in the wild. It is somewhat protected by its habitat, for limestone areas are not easy of access and one hopes that sufficient colonies survive where man cannot strip them. However, even sheer cliffs, one of its favoured habitats, do not seem to be sufficient to protect it. It grows on these at between 50–500 m elevation, lightly shaded by the crowns of trees growing at the base of the cliffs.

Paphiopedilum stonei is unlikely to be confused with any other species but is, nevertheless, quite variable in nature and several of the most unusual have received recognition at varietal rank. The most remarkable of these is var. *platyaenium* (Rchb.f.) Stein with broad petals 1.5 cm wide. Illustrations of this spectacular orchid are given by Warner &

P.J. Cribb

Fig. 40 (above). *Paphiopedilum stonei* growing in its natural habitat, a limestone hill near Kuching, Sarawak.

Fig. 41 (right). Close-up of a flower of *Paphiopedilum stonei*, with unusually narrow petals, cultivated at Kew.

P.J. Cribb

Fig. 42. A colony of healthy, non flowering plants of *Paphiopedilum stonei* in western Sarawak.

Williams (1897) in volume 11 of the *Orchid Album* (t. 496) and by
Warner (1878) in volume 3 of *Select Orchidaceous Plants* (t. 14). John
Day painted it in volume 23 of his *Scrapbook* (t. 63). He also illustrated
a remarkable flower in volume 12 (t. 40) in which one petal is normal
and the other of typical var. *platytaenium* form. This flower is preserved
in the Kew Herbarium. A piece of John Day's plant was later sold in
1881 to Sir Trevor Lawrence for 140 guineas and this plant survived and
flowered for many years before perishing some time before the First
World War.

Fig. 43. *Paphiopedilum stonei* from Veitch's Manual of Orchidaceous Plants,
1889.

Var. *candidum* (Masters) Pfitzer, which lacks purple pigment in the sepals, is another striking variant. Recently plants with reduced purple venation in the dorsal sepal and very broad leaves have been called var. *latifolium* Hort. These and var. *platytaenium* are best treated, in my opinion, as forms or cultivars since they have occurred as single plants or small numbers of plants introduced into cultivation.

The type of var. *stictopetalum,* described by M.W. Wood in 1977 and said to come from Waigeo Island off the west coast of New Guinea, is almost certainly of hybrid origin. The type specimen originated from a Javanese nursery which who had earlier sold P. × *jogjae,* a hybrid of *P. glanduliferum* × *glaucophyllum,* as a new species. I would suggest that var. *stictopetalum* is probably a man-made hybrid of *P. stonei* and the Himalayan species *P. spicerianum.* The artificial hybrid of this origin is called *P.* Alice.

Paphiopedilum stonei (Hook.) Stein, *Orchideenbuch* 487 (1892); Pfitzer in Engler, *Pflanzenr. Orch. Pleon.* 62 (1903). Type: Borneo, *Low* s.n., hort. Low (holotype K!).
Cypripedium stonei Hook. in *Curtis's Bot Mag.* 88: t. 5349 (1862) .
Cordula stonei (Hook.) Merrill in *Journ. Str. Roy. As. Soc. Spec. No.* 137 (1921).

DESCRIPTION. A *lithophytic herb. Leaves c.* 5, ligulate, rounded to obtuse, up to 70 cm long, 4.5 cm wide, green. *Inflorescence* arcuate, up to 70 cm long, usually 2–4-flowered; peduncle 17–35 cm, glabrous, purplish; bracts lanceolate, acute or acuminate, 3.5–5.5 cm long, 1.6–2.2 cm wide. *Flowers* up to 12 cm across; sepals white lined with dark maroon; petals yellow, lined and spotted maroon, somewhat flushed with maroon in apical half; lip pale yellow, flushed pink with darker veins; staminode yellow, pedicel and ovary 4–7 cm, glabrous. *Dorsal sepal* ovate, acuminate, 4 5–5.7 cm long, 3–4.4 cm wide. *Synsepal* elliptic-ovate, acuminate, 3.7–5 cm long, 2–3.4 cm wide. *Petals* arcuate-dependent, linear-tapering, 10–15 cm long, 0.4–0.75 cm wide, (rarely more, up to 2 cm broad in var. *platytaenium),* straight or twisted in apical half. *Lip* pointing forwards, grooved on back. 4.5–5.7 cm long, 2–2.8 cm wide. *Staminode* convex, subcircular, truncate or incised at apex, 14 mm long, 11 mm wide, margins coarsely hairy. 2n = 26.

DISTRIBUTION. Borneo (Sarawak only); 60–500 m altitude.

5. PAPHIOPEDILUM ROTHSCHILDIANUM

Baron Ferdinand de Rothschild, the eminent Victorian orchid grower, has the distinction of having the most spectacular orchid in the genus named after him. *P. rothschildianum* was introduced into cultivation by M. Jean Linden in May 1887 and, early the following year, by Messrs. Sander & Sons of St Albans. H.G. Reichenbach based his original description on a flower sent to him by Sander and said by the latter to have come from New Guinea. This appears to have been a deliberate attempt by Sander to mislead his competitors because we now know that the orchid is endemic to Mount Kinabalu in north-east Borneo. Linden had also cited the same origin and sold plants under the name *Cypripedium neo-guineense*, a name never validly published.

A. Lamb

R.S. Beaman

Fig. 45 (above). *Paphiopedilum rothschildianum* growing in its natural habitat on Mount Kinabalu.

Fig. 44 (opposite). *Paphiopedilum rothschildianum* growing in its natural habitat on Kinabalu where it can form large clumps.

C.L. Chan

Fig. 46. *Paphiopedilum rothschildianum* flowering in cultivation at the Poring Orchid Centre, Kinabalu Park.

Further confusion arose from the description of *Cypripedium elliottianum* by James O'Brien in November 1888 based on a Sander introduction and said to have been collected in the Philippines. O'Brien's statement that 'it is widely distinguished' from *C. rothschildianum* belies his description and the type collection at Kew which agree well with that species. Asher (1983) has recently resurrected *P. elliottianum* as possibly distinct but his case does not withstand critical scrutiny.

C.L. Chan

Fig. 47. A close-up of a flower of *Paphiopedilum rothschildianum*.

The name *P. elliottianum* has also recently been revived by Fowlie (1980a) and Braem (1988) for plants of Philippines origin now correctly ascribed to *P. adductum*. Unfortunately Fowlie's original identification has been taken up by many growers in ignorance of Asher's later correction.

The closest allies of *P. rothschildianum* are the New Guinea species *P. glanduliferum* and two recently described species: *P. adductum* from the Philippines and *P. supardii* from Kalimantan. It differs from all, however, in having longer petals held at an acute angle to the horizontal so that the flower often has a span of 24–30 cm. The staminode is also quite distinctive, narrow with a knee-like bend at the base, a bifid tip and a hairy base and sides.

Fig. 48. *Paphiopedilum rothschildianum* (as *Cypripedium elliotianum*) from Lindenia t. 436.

Of all the species in the genus, *P. rothschildianum* must be one of the rarest in nature. Despite extensive searching over a period of a hundred years, it has been located in only three sites on the lower slopes around Mount Kinabalu, in one of which it is certainly now extinct. These are the very places that are under the greatest threat from the destruction of their habitat by logging, mining and shifting agriculture. Even the precipitous nature of its habitat gives it precious little protection. It usually grows on ledges on steep slopes and cliffs of ultra-basic rock where it seems to thrive in the open as well as in shaded places. Individual plants can form sizeable clumps but it must be said that collectors could practically exterminate both populations in a relatively short time. Fortunately, *P. rothschildianum* grows only inside the Kinabalu Park and is afforded some protection. Growers should realise that, if offered wild-collected material, it would certainly be from a protected site and therefore its removal an illegal act.

Atwood (1985) has recently and elegantly demonstrated the significance of the strange staminode of *P. rothschildianum* in its pollination by syrphid flies. He suggests that the glandular hairs on the staminode

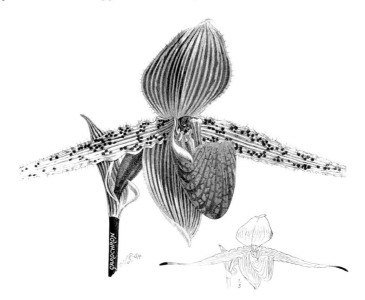

Fig. 49. *Paphiopedilum rothschildianum*, in B.S. Williams, The Orchid Grower's Manual, ed. 7 (1894).

Fig. 50. *Paphiopedilum rothschildianum* from Reichenbachia t. 61.

Fig. 51. *Paphiopedilum rothschildianum* flowering in its natural habitat in the Lohan Valley on Kinabalu. The population in this locality has been completely wiped out by a forest fire.

mimic an aphid colony, the normal brood site of the syrphid larvae. The staminode attracts females of the fly *Dideopsis aegrota*, to deposit their eggs on its surface. On alighting upon the staminode to lay their eggs, the flies sometimes fall into the lip. Their only possible exit is through the gap between the base of the lip and the column and the flies thereby pass beneath the stigma and pollinia. A visit to a second flower followed by a similar scenario will therefore effect pollination.

Paphiopedilum rothschildianum (Rchb.f.) Stein, *Orchideenbuch* 482 (1892); Pfitzer in Engler, *Pflanzenr. Orch. Pleon.* 59 (1903); Hook.f. in *Curtis's Bot. Mag.* 116: t. 7102 (1890). Type: hort. *Sander* (holotype W!).
Cypripedium rothschildianum Rchb.f. in *Gard. Chron.* ser. 3, 3: 457 (1888).
C. elliotianum O'Brien in *Gard.Chron.* ser. 3, 4: 501 (1888). Type: hort. *Sander* (holotype K!).
P. elliottianum (O'Brien) Stein, *Orchideenbuch* 466 (1892).
P. rothschildianum (Rchb.f.) Stein var. *elliottianum* (O'Brien) Pfitzer in Engler, *Pflanzenr. Orch. Pleon.* 59 (1903).
Cordula rothschildiana (Rchb.f.) Merrill in *Journ. Str. Br. Roy. As. Soc. Spec. No.* 137 (1921).

DESCRIPTION. A *terrestrial* or *lithophytic herb* often growing in large clumps. *Leaves* several, linear to narrowly oblanceolate, acute, up to 60 cm long, 4–5 cm wide, sparsely ciliate at base, green. *Inflorescence* 2- to 4-flowered, erect; peduncle up to 45 cm long, purple, shortly pubescent; bracts ovate-elliptic, obtuse, up to 5.5 cm long, ciliate and hairy on mid-vein, pale green or yellow, purple-striped. *Flowers* very large, 14–30 cm in diameter; ovary up to 7.5 cm long, pale green sparsely spotted purple, glabrous. *Dorsal sepal* ovate, acute to acuminate, 6–6.6 cm long, 3.3–4.8 cm wide, ivory-white or yellow with maroon veins. *Synsepal* similar but smaller, 5.7–6 cm long, 3.3–4 cm wide. *Petals* narrowly tapering to rounded apex, 8–14 cm long, 0.7–1.4 cm wide, ciliate, papillose towards apex, yellow or ivory-white marked with maroon. *Lip* subporrect, grooved on back, 5–5.7 cm long, 2–2.2 cm wide, golden, heavily purple-suffused; side-lobes not auricular. *Staminode* linear, bifid at apex, geniculate, 14–16 mm long, 4–5 mm wide, densely glandular-pubescent on margins and at base, pale yellow-green. 2n = 26.

DISTRIBUTION. Borneo: Sabah only; 600–1200 m altitude.

6. PAPHIOPEDILUM SUPARDII

I n plant size and habit, *P. supardii* could easily be mistaken for *P. rothschildianum*. Its lip is also similar but it differs in having much shorter, slightly incurved and half-twisted, yellow-green petals, boldly marked with brownish maroon, and a much reduced subquadrate staminode which does not cover the stigma or the lateral anthers.

Paphiopedilum supardii is most closely allied to *P. rothschildianum*. Its reduced staminode is similar to that of *P. adductum* but, in that species, the petals are much longer, straight and tapering to the apex.

Fig. 52. A close-up of a flower of *Paphiopedilum supardii* exhibited at the Royal Horticultural Society in London. (Photo: P.J. Cribb)

Fig. 53. An inflorescence of *Paphiopedilum supardii,* flowering in cultivation at a nursery in East Java.

P.J. C

The first mention of this strange orchid was made by W.F. van Hell in 1938 in the Dutch journal *De Orchidee*. This has been overlooked by subsequent authors because van Hell referred his plant to the New Guinea species *P. praestans* (= *P. glanduliferum*). Despite asserting that his plant came from Dutch New Guinea, the excellent black and white photograph clearly shows a plant of *P. supardii*. Then first clue to its actual origin came when Dr Eduard de Vogel (Fig. 14, page 13) of the University of Leiden rediscovered it on an expedition to south-east Kalimantan in 1972. He also published a photograph of it, under the name *P. 'victoria'*, in *Panda* Nieuws in 1975.

Schoser and Deelder (1971) intended describing it shortly afterwards as a new species, '*P. devogelii*', but did not eventually do so although the name later became widely used amongst orchid growers. It was first introduced into cultivation in 1983 when plants from Kalimantan were sent to Liem Khe Wie of Lawang, east Java. A quantity of plants have been sold in the USA, Australia and Europe by him as '*P. devogelii*'. Unfortunately, instead of validating that name, Braem & Loeb (1985) described this species as *P. supardii* without checking to see if their specimen was the same as that collected by de Vogel. The name used by them refers to the collector of their type material.

Paphiopedilum supardii G. Braem & Löb in *Die Orchidee* 36(4): separate & 142 (1985). Type: Borneo, Kalimantan, *Supardi* in *Braem* GB 585 (holotype SCHL).

P. praestans sensu van Hell in De Orchidee July 1938: 157 (1938), *non* (Rchb.f.) Pfitzer

P. 'victoria' de Vogel in *Panda Nieuws* 12: 117 (1975), *nom. nud.*

DESCRIPTION. An erect *lithophytic herb* with a very short stem. *Leaves* 7–9, arranged in a fan, coriaceous, suberect, ligulate, rounded at unequally bilobed apex, 22–55 cm long, 3.5–5.5 cm wide, dark green, keeled on lower surface. Inflorescence erect, 3- to 6-flowered, 30–45 cm long; peduncle 20–30 cm long; bracts large, elliptic, acute, up to 5.2 cm long, pale yellow-green, veined with purple. *Flowers* appearing deformed, pale yellow to yellowish-green; dorsal sepal with brownish purple lines; petals spotted with red-maroon; lip yellow or white flushed pale to darker red-brown with purplish veins; staminode yellow with marginal brown hairs; pedicel and ovary up to 4.5 cm long, brown-maroon. *Dorsal sepal* ovate, acute or acuminate, 2.5–5.5 cm long, 2.4–2.6 cm wide. *Synsepal* ovate, acuminate, 2.5–5.5 cm long, *c.* 2.2 cm wide. *Petals* deflexed, contorted-twisted, linear-tapering, obtuse, once-twisted in apical half, 8–9 cm long, 0.7–0.9 cm wide. *Lip* apically broad but rather pointed in side view, 4–5 cm long, 1.5–1.8 cm wide. *Staminode* geniculate, subquadrate in front view, 8 mm long, 8–9 mm across, pilose on each side, not covering anthers on each side of stigmatic stalk.

DISTRIBUTION. Borneo: south-east Kalimantan only; growing on limestone rocks in leaf-mould filled hollows in half shade; 600–960 m. altitude.

7. PAPHIOPEDILUM LOWII var. LOWII

*P*aphiopedilum lowii is the most widespread of the multi-flowered species, found throughout the Malay Peninsula, Sumatra, Java, Borneo and the Celebes (Sulawesi). It is also one of the few epiphytic species in the genus although it may also occasionally be found growing on rocks.

Hugh Low (epigraph, page v), of the famous nursery firm of Messrs. Low & Sons of Clapton, discovered this species in 1846 in North Borneo (now Sabah) on his famous expedition to Mount Kinabalu and *P. lowii* was named in his honour by John Lindley in the following year. *P. lowii* was still to be found on the Pinosok Plateau area of Mount Kinabalu as late as 1980 but it is doubtful if it still survives there since the conversion of the site to farming and a golf course in 1982.

A. Lamb

Fig. 54. *Paphiopedilum lowii* cultivated in the Mountain Garden, Kinabalu Park.

Fig. 55. A close-up of a flower of *Paphiopedilum lowii*. Note the basal protuberance of the staminode.

C.L. Chan

P.J. Cribb

Despite its wide distribution, *P. lowii* is relatively uniform in the shape of its floral segments and coloration. Plants from 1400–1600 m on Mount Kinabalu have leaves that are broader than usual, 4–5 cm wide, and rather deeper coloured flowers. The lip in some forms can be short and broad at the apex with the veins distinctly sunken whilst the degree of spotting and spot size on the petals can also vary. I can see no discontinuities in the variation patterns of this species in Malaya, Sumatra, Java and Borneo to warrant recognition of infraspecific taxa in *P. lowii*, other than the albino form mentioned below. However, in Sulawesi a small-flowered plant with boldly marked flowers was recently described as *P. richardianum* by John Beaman and James Asher. Koopowitz (1995) and Gruss (1997) have both considered this should be better considered as variety of *P. lowii*, and I am inclined to agree that it differs from the typical *P. lowii* in too few characters to warrant its recognition at a higher rank.

Fig. 57. *Paphiopedilum lowii* in B.S. Williams, the *Orchid Growers Manual*, ed. 7 (1894).

Fig. 56 (opposite). A large plant of *P. lowii* growing in a riverside tree in the Apokayan highlands, Kalimantan, Indonesian Borneo.

It is most closely allied to the Philippines species of *P. haynaldianum* from which it can be readily recognised by the lack of spotting on the more ovate-elliptic dorsal sepal, the narrower petals with smaller more numerous spotting in the basal half, the shorter broader lip and the broader staminode, three-toothed at the apex. These distinctions and the geographical isolation of *P. haynaldianum* seems sufficient to keep it separate from *P. lowii*.

Paphiopedilum lowii can be found growing at altitudes up to about 1600 m in riverine, lower montane and montane rain forest either as an epiphyte on the trunks and branches of trees or as a lithophyte in moss- or humus-filled hollows of rocks (especially limestone) and of boulders. In these areas the rainfall is usually high particularly under the influence in the summer of the south-west monsoon when the temperature can rise to over 30°C (86°F) to 20°C (68°F) at night. The winters are usually drier and cooler with the night temperature dropping to *c.* 12°C (54°F). The epiphytic habit is such that, even in the wettest months, the plant will dry out rapidly as soon as the sun hits it. In nature, *P. lowii* flowers from April until June.

I have recently described an albino variant of *P. lowii* that has been collected at least twice from the Upper Rajang River in Sarawak as var. *aureum*. It was originally collected by Mr Yii Pua Ching of the Sarawak Forest Department in 1989 and more recently by John and Teofilia Beaman. I am here reducing this occasional mutation to the rank of form (see below).

Paphiopedilum lowii (Lindl.) Stein, *Orchideenbuch* 476 (1982). Type: Borneo, *Low* (holotype K!).
Cypripedium lowii Lindl. in *Gard. Chron.* 1847: 765 (1847).
Cordula lowii (Lindl.) Rolfe in *Orchid Rev.* 20: 2 (1912). (As *C. lowiana.*)

DESCRIPTION. An *epiphytic* or rarely *lithophytic herb. Leaves* 4–6, linear-ligulate, unequally roundly bilobed at apex, 22–40 cm long, 2.8–6 cm wide, mid-green. *Inflorescence* erect-arcuate, 3–7-flowered; peduncle green, mottled purple, shortly pubescent, up to 50 cm long; bracts elliptic, obtuse, 2–4.5 cm long, 2.2 cm wide, yellow, marked with purple, pubescent. *Flowers* 9–14 cm across; pedicel and ovary 4.5–7 cm long, greenish, pubescent, long rostrate. *Dorsal sepal* elliptic-ovate, obtuse,

3.3–5.5 cm long, 2.5–3.2 cm wide, undulate and ciliate on margins, pale green, mottled dull purple in basal half, with recurved basal margins. *Synsepal* elliptic, obtuse, 2.2–4 cm, 2-keeled on outer surface, pale green. *Petals* often once-twisted in middle, spathulate, subacute to obtuse, 5–9 cm long, 1.5–2 cm wide, ciliate, pale yellow with a purple apical third and maroon-spotted in basal two-thirds. *Lip* 3.5–4 cm long, 2.7 cm wide, dull ochre-brown. *Staminode* obovate, apically three-toothed with a long erect hook at the base, 10 mm long, 7 mm wide, pale ochre to brownish green. 2n = 26.

DISTRIBUTION. Peninsular Malaysia, Sumatra, Java, Borneo and Sulawesi (var. *richardianum*) ; 250–1600 m altitude.

forma **aureum** (Cribb) Cribb **stat. nov.** (Fig. 58)
   P. lowii var. *aureum* Cribb in Orchid Review 98: 109, fig. 74 (1990).

DISTRIBUTION. Borneo: Sarawak only.

Fig. 58. *P. lowii* f. *aureum* from the Bakun area, Sarawak.

73

8. PAPHIOPEDILUM LOWII var. LYNNIAE

Leslie Garay (1997) recently described *P. lynniae*, based upon a cultivated specimen said to have come from Borneo but otherwise of
unknown provenance. It is closely allied to *P. lowii* and, in my opinion,
does not warrant recognition at specific rank. He compared it with *P.
lowii* but it differs in having glabrous sepals, ovary, pedicel, bracts,
peduncle and rachis, a keeled dorsal sepal and two-keeled synsepal, both
lightly spotted in their basal halves, and a staminode with three equal
apical teeth and a long basal umbo. It may be that its relationship to *P.
lowii* is similar to that between *P. parishii* and *P. dianthum* in mainland
South-east Asia, but its isolated occurrence in cultivation and lack of
exact provenance suggests that it is more likely a variation of *P. lowii*,
which is a widespread species in Borneo. I am, therefore, tentatively
following Gruss & Röth in reducing it to varietal status within *P. lowii*.
Certainly, more needs to be known about its distribution and natural
variation.

var. **lynniae** *(Garay) Gruss & Röth* in Orchidee 48: 72 (1997).
P. lynniae Garay in *Lindleyana* 11: 233 (1996). Type: Borneo, exact
provenance unknown, cult. L. Wellenstein (holotype AMES!, isotype
K!).

DESCRIPTION. Differs from the typical variety in having glabrous ovary
and sepals, two prominent keels on the back of the synsepal, and a
staminode in which the central apical tooth is as long as the side teeth.

DISTRIBUTION. Borneo, without exact locality.

9. PAPHIOPEDILUM BULLENIANUM
var. BULLENIANUM

*P*aphiopedilum bullenianum is a widespread species in Borneo
found growing in a variety of habitats. At sea-level in Sarawak it
reportedly grows in moss and leaf-litter on the stilt-roots of
mangroves. However, in my experience it grows in leaf-litter in shade on
the forested slopes of valleys through which streams run down to the

coast. At higher altitudes of 700–950 m it also grows in leaf-litter on steep slopes and wet moss-covered rocks in shade of low forest.

Paphiopedilum bullenianum and its allies present one of the most complex taxonomic problems in the genus. Altogether, around eight or more specific names are involved and many of these are still freely used for plants in cultivation. In addition to *P. bullenianum*, the main names involved are *P. amabile*, *P. robinsonii*, *P. linii*, *P. johorense*, *P. celebesense* and *P. tortipetalum*. Of these, the last four have been described since 1966 and have further confused an already complex problem.

H.G. Reichenbach described *Cypripedium bullenianum* in 1865 based on a Bornean plant sent him by Messrs. Low & Co. of Clapton, naming it in honour of Mr Bullen their orchid grower. Reichenbach distinguished it by its white and green tessellated leaves which he compared with those of *C. venustum* and green and purple-marked flower which resembled a small *C. insigne*. It is, in fact, closely allied to *P. appletonianum* and to *P. hookerae*. Its differences from the former have already been mentioned but it can readily be confused with the latter when not in

Fig. 59. A close-up of a flower of *Paphiopedilum bullenianum* cultivated at Kew.

Fig. 60. *Paphiopedilum bullenianum*. (Painting by C.L. Chan).

flower. It differs, however, in having a less pubescent flower with a lip that is less flared at the mouth and less inflated at the apex, the narrower petals and smaller, narrower subrhombic glabrous staminode with more or less parallel apical lateral teeth.

The type of *P. amabile* was collected by Hallier in 1893 in the Klamm Mountains of Borneo at 700–950 m altitude. He described it in 1895 comparing it with the tessellated-leaved species *P. javanicum, P. mastersianum, P. dayanum, P. hookerae* and *P. virens* but not *P. bullenianum* of which he was apparently unaware. Examination of the type of *P. amabile* shows it to be identical with *P. bullenianum* in all critical vegetative and floral features.

Paphiopedilum linii was described by Gustav Schoser in 1966 based on material collected 10 miles (16 km) from Kuching in Sarawak where the plants were growing in accumulated leaf litter on the roots of mangroves. He named it in honour of its discoverer Mrs Phyllis Sheridan-Lea (also known as Mrs Lin). The author distinguished it from *P. bullenianum* by its staminode which is distally bi- and not tridentate. Examination of several specimens of *P. bullenianum* indicates that the degree of development of the central tooth of the staminode is variable and that *P. linii* falls within the range of variation seen in *P. bullenianum*. Plants of *P. linii* which I have seen in cultivation have petals which are relatively well spotted in their basal half but, again, this is a very variable character in *P. bullenianum*.

Henry Ridley, famous for his introduction of rubber into Malaya, described a slipper orchid, first collected in 1911 on Gunung Tahan in peninsular Malaysia, as *Cypripedium robinsonii*. This he compared with the widespread Malayan species *P. barbatum* but not with the Bornean *P. bullenianum*. It is certainly very close to the latter, with boldly mottled leaves and a flower that differs only in the spreading apical lateral teeth of the staminode. However, examination of an isotype at Kew has shown that the staminode teeth do not spread in every flower. Ridley described its stems as stoloniferous and Holttum (1957) in the *Orchids of Malaya* says that they often extend more than a foot (30 cm) in length. The production of elongated rhizomes is dependent in many orchids upon environmental factors; *P. druryi* and *P. bougainvilleanum* produce long rhizomes in nature but seldom in cultivation.

A. Lamb

Fig. 61. A close-up of a flower of *P. bullenianum.*

Paphiopedilum johorense, collected by Fedderson on Gunung Panti in Jahore State in the southern part of peninsular Malaysia and at a lower altitude than *P. robinsonii*, is morphologically similar, particularly in its staminode shape and general floral morphology. Plants collected by Paul Mattes (*Orchid Digest* 49(1985): 233) on Pulau Tioman, just off the east coast of Johore, agree well with the type of *P. johorense* as illustrated by Yap & Lee (1972). I do not consider the slight differences in staminode apex to be taxonomically significant and consider all these species conspecific with *P. bullenianum.*

The most recently recognised of this group is the Sumatran *P. tortipetalum* which Fowlie described in 1985 based on a collection from the Barisan Mountains. He compares it with *P. johorense* distinguishing it on minor characters of petal attitude, the shape of the petal and lip apices and the leaf mottling. I have dissected another flower from the same collection as the type and its staminode is identical with that of Bornean *P. bullenianum* material examined. It also has the boldly marked foliage, short dorsal sepal and blunt petals of *P. bullenianum* and I therefore include it in that species.

In many ways the peninsular Malaysian and Sumatran plants are intermediate in floral morphology between Bornean *P. bullenianum* and *P. appletonianum.*

The plant illustrated by Fowlie (1974c) as *P. robinsonii* does not agree with the type material of that species. It differs in having a shortly hairy staminode with short or obscure lateral apical teeth and a longer mid-tooth. The lip is reminiscent of *P. hookerae* in shape and has a ciliate apical margin quite unlike that of *P. bullenianum*. The leaves are, however, boldly marked and, almost indistinguishable from that species. I have seen several preserved collections of this entity, none from a wild source. Whilst I do not rule out the possibility of '*P. robinsonii*' sensu Fowlie being a distinct species it seems possible that it is a hybrid of *P. bullenianum* with another species, possibly *P. hookerae*. Until further material of known provenance is available a sensible solution to this problem is unlikely.

Paphiopedilum celebesense (as *P. celebesensis*) was described by Fowlie & Birk in 1980 based on a collection by the latter from east of Rantepao in central Sulawesi. They distinguished it from *P. bullenianum* by the fewer spots on the margin of petals, the lack of a prominent emarginate apex to the lip and the convergent apical lateral teeth of the lip. These features are all variable in *P. bullenianum* and the staminode of *P. celebesense* can be exactly matched in Bornean specimens. Karasawa (1979) gives the chromosome number of *P. celebesense* as 2n = 42 and this together with the minor floral differences seem just about sufficient to warrant its recognition as a variety of *P. bullenianum*.

Birk (1983) used the name *P. 'ceramensis'* for plants from Ceram in the Moluccas. this name is not validly published and, from examination of living material and published photographs, I unhesitatingly include it in *P. bullenianum* var. *celebesense*.

On the Indonesian islands of Sulawesi and Ceram, var. *celebesense* grows on north facing slopes in lightly shaded places under ferns with the roots in deep humus and mosses in association with *Nepenthes*, *Selaginella* and ferns at 950 m altitude (Birk 1983).

Paphiopedilum bullenianum (Rchb.f.) Pfitzer in Engler, *Bot. Jahrb.* 19: 40 (1894): Birk, *Paph. Grower's Man.* 65 (1983). Type: Borneo, hort. *Low* (holotype W!).
Cypripedium bullenianum Rchb.f. in *Bot. Zeit.* 23: 99 (1865).

C. hookerae Rchb.f. var. *bullenianum* (Rchb.f.) Veitch, *Man.* 4: 32 (1880).

Paphiopedilum hookerae (Rchb.f.) Stein var. *bullenianum* (Reichb.f.) Kerch., *Orch.* 454 (1894).

P. amabile Hallier in *Naturk. Tijdschr. Ned. Ind.* 54: 450 (1895). Type: Borneo, Kalimantan, *Hallier* (holotype BO!).

Cypripedium hookerae Rchb.f. var. *amabile* (Hallier) Kränzl., *Orchid.* 1: 59 (1897).

Cordula bulleniana (Rchb.f.) Rolfe in *Orchid Rev.* 20: 2 (1912).

C. amabile (Hallier) Merrill in *Journ.* Str. Br. Roy. As. Soc. Spec. No. 135 (1921).

Cypripedium robinsonii Ridley in *Journ. Fed. Malay States Mus.* 6: 183 (1915). Type: Malaya, G. Tahan, *Robinson* (holotype SING!).

Paphiopedilum robinsonii (Ridley) Ridley, *Fl. Malay Penins.* 4: 232 (1924).

P. linii Schoser in *Die Orchidee* 16: 181 (1966). Type: Sarawak, cult. Tuebingen B.G. ex *Sheridan-Lea* s.n. (holotype TUB!).

P. johorense Fowlie & Yap in *Orchid Dig.* 36: 73 (1972). Type: western Malaysia, Johore, *Fedderson* (holotype SING!).

P. tortipetalum Fowlie in *Orchid Dig.* 49: 153 (1985). Type: Sumatra, Barisan Mountains, cult. Los Angeles Arb. (holotype UCLA!).

DESCRIPTION. A *terrestrial herb. Leaves* 6–8, elliptic, oblanceolate or oblong-elliptic, tridenticulate at obtuse apex, 7–14 cm long, 2.5–4 cm wide, boldly tessellated dark and pale green above, sometimes flushed with purple below. *Inflorescence* erect, 1-flowered; peduncle 20–55 cm long, green and purple, pubescent; bract ovate-elliptic, acute 1.5–2.1 cm long, ciliate. *Flower* up to 9.5 cm across; sepals white with green veins; often dark purple-marked at base of dorsal; petals green at base, purple above, with dark maroon-black spotting on margins and sometimes on the lamina of basal half; lip ochre to greenish; ovary and pedicel 4–6 cm long, pubescent. *Dorsal sepal* usually concave, ovate, acute, 2.4–3 cm long, 1.4–2.2 cm wide, shortly pubescent on outer surface. *Synsepal* lanceolate, acute, 1.9–2.5 cm long, 1–1.5 cm wide. *Petals* spathulate to oblanceolate, obtuse, 3.8–5.2 cm long, 0.9–1.4 cm wide, ciliate. *Lip* 3–4 cm long, emarginate at apex. *Staminode* subcircular to subrhombic, deeply incised at apex, 6–9 mm long, 6–8 mm wide, lateral teeth subparallel to spreading, ± with a short tooth in apical sinus. $2n = 40$.

DISTRIBUTION. Borneo, Sumatra and peninsular Malaysia; sea-level to 1850 m altitude.

10. PAPHIOPEDILUM HOOKERAE var. HOOKERAE

This beautiful orchid was another of Hugh Low's introductions from Borneo for Messrs. Low & Sons. H.G. Reichenbach described it in *Curtis's Botanical Magazine* in 1863 based on a plant from the Low importation flowered by W. Marshall of Enfield. He named it in honour of Lady Hooker, the wife of Sir William, then Director of Kew. Reichenbach graphically described it as having "Flowers of *Cypripedium hirsutissimum* and leaves of *Phalaenopsis schillerianum* [*sic*], or nearly so". H.G. Reichenbach in the account that follows the description compared it with *P. javanicum*, *P. barbatum* and *P. purpuratum*. However, it is now considered most closely allied to the widespread *P. bullenianum* and to the Sulawesi species *P. sangii* with both of which it shares boldly marked leaves and a similar flower. It differs from the former in its almost circular, larger staminode, and from the latter in its acute dorsal sepal, petal shape and colour, and its purplish brown rather than greenish cream staminode.

For many years, *P. hookerae* was considered to be one of the rarest and most prized of all the species. Following Low's collection, Messrs. Veitch introduced it from southern Sarawak in 1865 where it grows on limestone at 300–450 m altitude, and Messrs. Sander & Sons imported it in some quantity in the 1880s. Following these importations of the nineteenth century, it was even considered by some to be extinct. However, a plant imported from Sarawak in late 1972 by a Japanese grower, Fuminasa Sugiyama, which flowered in the collection of George Kennedy in 1975, proved to be of *P. hookerae*. Shortly afterwards a Japanese engineer, Hali Handoyo, discovered it in western Kalimantan. Fowlie (1981) describes the habitat where Handoyo discovered it at 600–800 m elevation near the summits of weathered sandstone hills. *P. hookerae* grows there at the edges of steep cliffs under an open canopy of trees and in leaf litter at the base of trees and in crevices where there is constant seepage of water. Fowlie also reports that two leaf types are found there, plants with, respectively, grey-green and grass-green mottled leaves. The plants flower in March and April in this locality.

Paphiopedilum hookerae (Rchb.f.) Stein, *Orchideenbuch* 470 (1892); Fowlie in *Orchid Dig*. 39: 164 (1975) & 45: 165 (1981). Type: Borneo, *Low* s.n. (holotype W!).

Cypripedium hookerae Rchb.f. in *Curtis's Bot. Mag.* 89: t. 5362 (1863) & *Xenia Orchid.* 2: 125, t. 141 (1874).

DESCRIPTION. A *terrestrial herb. Leaves* 5–6, oblong-elliptic, obtuse and minutely tridentate at apex, 7–23 cm long, 2.7–5 cm wide, boldly tessellated dark and light green on upper surface. *Inflorescence* 1-flowered; peduncle to 50 cm long, purple, white-pubescent; bract lanceolate, acute, 20–30 mm long, 14 mm wide, pale brownish, pubescent. *Flower c.* 8 cm across; ovary 5 cm long, bright green, pubescent. *Dorsal sepal* ovate, acute, 3–4 cm long, 2.3–2.9 cm wide, with reflexed basal margins, cream flushed bright green in centre. *Synsepal* elliptic, bidentate, 2–3 cm long, 1.4–1.6 cm wide, pale yellow. *Petals* deflexed, half twisted in middle, spathulate, subacute, 4–5.5 cm long, 1.5–2.2 cm wide, ciliate, pale green, heavily spotted brown in basal two-thirds, margins and apical third purple. *Lip* 3.8–4.2 cm long, 1.7 cm wide, brown, brown-warted on side lobes, ciliate on slightly reflexed apical margin. *Staminode* circular, apically excised, 10 mm long and wide; side-lobes at apex incurved-falcate. 2n = 28.

DISTRIBUTION. Borneo: Sarawak and western Kalimantan; 150–600 m altitude.

Fig. 62. *Paphiopedilum hookerae* var. *hookerae.*

11. PAPHIOPEDILUM HOOKERAE
var. VOLONTEANUM

This attractive orchid was originally described as *Cypripedium hookerae* var. *volonteanum* by Robert Rolfe in 1890 based on a plant collected in Sarawak by Hugh Low and introduced by Messrs. Low & Sons of Clapton. Messrs. Sander & Sons introduced it at about the same time. Rolfe compared it with typical *P. hookerae* stating that its "'leaves are proportionately narrower…, the petals broader and more obtuse, the lip a little constricted below the horizontal mouth and the staminode quite orbicular, without notches". The leaves are also purple-mottled beneath and, together with their narrowness, these are the most readily accessible distinguishing features. The petals and staminode are unreliable distinguishing features being very variable from plant to plant and overlapping with *P. hookerae*. Pfitzer raised Rolfe's variety to specific

C.L. Chan

Fig. 63. Close-up of flower of *P. hookerae* var. *volonteanum.*

C.L. Chan

Fig. 64 (above). Side view of a flower of
Paphiopedilum hookerae var. *volonteanum* cultivated
at the Poring Orchid Centre, Kinabalu Park.

Fig. 65 (opposite above) *Paphiopedilum hookerae* var. *volonteanum* growing on
the lower slopes of Mount Kinabalu.

Fig. 66 (opposite below). Close-up of a flower of *Paphiopedilum hookerae* var.
volonteanum.

T.J. Barkman

T.J. Barkman

rank as *Paphiopedilum volonteanum* in 1903. However, recent collections in Sabah have shown a considerable range of petal, lip and staminode shape and of leaf width and purple-mottling beneath the leaves in this taxon. A recent collection from the lower west slopes of Kinabalu had leaves as broad as *P. hookerae* and mottled with purple only at the base (A. Lamb, pers. comm.). The Sabahan plants usually have a large flower on a tall peduncle but the petal apex can vary from subacute to obtuse and tridentate. Our better knowledge of the variability of *P. volonteanum* reinforces Rolfe's view that the latter is a variety of *P. hookerae* rather than a distinct species.

The range of altitude over which var. *volonteanum* has been collected is remarkable. It has recently been found on Mount Kinabalu growing on a granite scree under the shade of bushes at 2100 m altitude. I have found it growing in a colony of a few hundred plants along a ridge top at 900 m in deep leaf litter and in the shade of 15 m tall trees, while Sheila Collenette (pers. comm.) collected it at 200 m, growing under *Gymnostoma* trees near a waterfall in light shade on rocks and tree roots.

Paphiopedilum hookerae (Rchb.f.) Stein, *Orchideenbuch* 470 (1892); Fowlie in *Orchid Dig.* 39: 164 (1975) & 45: 165 (1981). Type: Borneo, *Low* s.n. (holotype W!).
   Cypripedium hookerae Rchb.f. in *Curtis's Bot. Mag.* 89: t. 5362 (1863) & *Xenia Orchid.* 2: 125, t. 141 (1874).

var. **volonteanum** (Sander ex Rolfe) Kerch., *Orch.* 456 (1894).
   Cypripedium hookerae Rchb.f. var. *volonteanum* Sander ex Rolfe in *Gard. Chron.* ser. 3, 8: 66 (1890). Type: Borneo, *Low* (holotype K!).
   Paphiopedilum volonteanum (Sander ex Rolfe) Pfitzer in Engler, *Pflanzenr. Orch. Pleon.* 80 (1903); Fowlie in *Orchid Dig.* 39: 170 (1975).

DESCRIPTION. Differs from the typical variety in having proportionately narrower leaves, purple-spotted below, broader and more obtuse petals and the lip a little constricted below the horizontal mouth. The degree of purple mottling on the underside of the leaves varies greatly. This variety occurs over a surprisingly wide altitudinal range.

DISTRIBUTION. Borneo (Sabah only); 60–2100 m altitude.

12. PAPHIOPEDILUM LAWRENCEANUM

*P*aphiopedilum lawrenceanum is one of the most important parental species in slipper orchid breeding, notable for its large, deeply coloured flower and large, flat dorsal sepal. It was introduced from Borneo by F.W. Burbidge (Fig. 11), one of Messrs. Veitch's collectors and was described by H.G. Reichenbach in 1878 who

Fig. 67. *Paphiopedilum lawrenceanum* from B.S. Williams' The Orchid Growers Manual, 1894.

Fig. 68. *Paphiopedilum lawrenceanum* var. *viride* from Lindenia t. 546.

dedicated it to Sir Trevor Lawrence, the eminent Victorian orchid grower and President of the Royal Horticultural Society. Its exact distribution in Borneo is something of a mystery. Burbidge visited Mount Kinabalu, Brunei and Labuan, but *P. lawrenceanum* has never been seen by others in any of these places. In Frederick Sander's correspondence, Ericcson mentions finding a fine tessellated-leaved species of slipper orchid on the Limbang River in Sarawak and this may well have been this species.

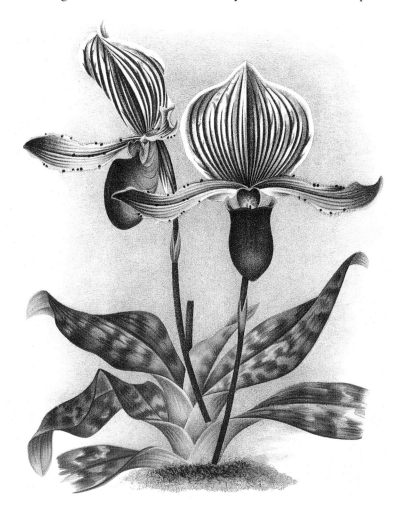

Fig. 69. *Paphiopedilum lawrenceanum* var. *trieuanum* from Lindenia t. 42.

Fig. 70. *Paphiopedilum lawrenceanum* var. *hyeanum* from Lindenia t. 42.

Paphiopedilum lawrenceanum is closely related to *P. barbatum* and *P. callosum* from mainland South-east Asia and to *P. hennisianum* from the Philippines. It is distinguished from the former by its boldly tessellated leaves, the spreading petals which bear dark maroon warts on both upper and lower margins, its bold and very large dorsal sepal and rather differently shaped staminode. From *P. hennisianum*, it differs in having a much larger, differently coloured flower in which the dorsal sepal is relatively much larger and the petals are not markedly reflexed.

Paphiopedilum lawrenceanum has been considered by Wood (1976) a subspecies of *P. barbatum*. It differs, however, in having a larger flower with a larger dorsal sepal and petals spotted along both margins.

The type of *P. nigritum* (Rchb.f.) Pfitzer was said to have been imported from Borneo by The New Bulb Co. of Colchester. It has a small, darker-coloured flower than *P. lawrenceanum* and the petals have warts only on the upper margins. It is very close to *P. barbatum* and Pfitzer (1903) in Engler's *Pflanzenreich* treated it as a variety of that species. I cannot but agree with Pfitzer's conclusion.

Fig. 71. Close-up of a flower of *Paphiopedilum lawrenceanum* cultivated at Royal Botanic Gardens, Kew.

Recent introductions under the name *P. nigritum* (such as that illustrated in the *Orchid Digest* 32: 125, 1968) are small-flowered forms of *P. lawrenceanum* and not true *P. nitritum*.

Paphiopedilum lawrenceanum is not at all common in nature as evidenced by its very spasmodic introductions into cultivation. According to Veitch (1889) it is found in primary forest in small colonies growing in deep leaf litter and, less commonly, on mossy limestone rocks.

Fig. 72. *Paphiopedilum lawrenceanum* 'Hockbridgense', exhibited by Sir T. Lawrence and painted by Nellie Roberts in 20th March, 1902.

Several varieties of *P. lawrenceanum* have been recognised. The most outstanding of these is var. *hyeanum* Rchb.f. (Fig. 71), an albino first flowered by the Belgian nurseryman, Jean Linden, in 1885. Var. *atrorubens* Rolfe, flowered for the first time by O.O. Wrigley of Bury in 1894, has a richly coloured flower, slightly smaller than the typical, with a deep purple lip and purple-suffused dorsal sepal. It is probably close to var. *coloratum* Hort. in its colouring. These and other varieties listed by Pfitzer (1903) are best treated as cultivars.

Paphiopedilum lawrenceanum (Rchb.f.) Pfitzer in *Pringsh. Jahrb. Wiss. Bot.* 19: 163 (1888) & in Engler, *Pflanzenr. Orch. Pleon.* 94 (1903); Stein, *Orchideenbuch* 473 (1892). Type: Borneo, cult. Sander, *Burbidge* s.n. (holotype W!).
Cypripedium lawrenceanum Rchb.f. in *Gard. Chron.* n.s. 10: 748 (1878).
Cordula lawrenceana (Rchb.f.) Merrill in *J. Str. Br. Roy. As. Soc. Spec. No.* 136 (1921).
Paphiopedilum barbatum (Lindl.) Pfitzer subsp. *lawrenceanum* (Rchb.f.) M. Wood in *Orchid Rev.* 84: 352 (1976).

DESCRIPTION. A *terrestrial herb. Leaves* 5–6, elliptic to narrowly elliptic, acute to obtuse, minutely tridenticulate at apex, up to 19 cm long, 4–6.5 cm wide, dark green mottled with yellow-green above, pale green below. *Inflorescence* 1-flowered; peduncle up to 31 cm long, pubescent, maroon; bract ovate, acute, 16–20 cm long, green veined maroon. *Flower* large, up to 11.5 cm across; ovary 4–6.5 cm, pubescent, green with maroon ridges. *Dorsal sepal* broadly ovate-subcircular, obtuse, *c.* 6–6.2 cm long and wide, often with lateral margins slightly reflexed, white with veins maroon above and green below. *Synsepal* narrowly lanceolate, obtuse to emarginate at apex, 4 cm long, 1.4 cm wide, white flushed green and veined maroon. *Petals* ligulate, subacute, at right angles to the dorsal sepal, *c.* 6 cm long, 1.1 cm wide, maroon-warted and purple-ciliate on both margins, green with a purple apex. *Lip* with incurved and maroon-warted side-lobes, 5.5–6.5 cm long, 2.8–3.2 cm wide, green heavily overlaid with dull maroon, maroon-spotted within. *Staminode* lunate, 9–11 mm long, 14.5 mm wide, green with darker green veining and a purple margin. 2n = 36.

DISTRIBUTION. Borneo (Sarawak and ?Brunei); 300–450 m altitude.

13. PAPHIOPEDILUM DAYANUM

The name of this orchid celebrates the eminent Victorian orchid grower and painter John Day (Fig. 13) of Tottenham (which lies on the northern outskirts of London). Day sent flowers of a stream of new species to H.G. Reichenbach (Fig. 12) , who reciprocated by naming several in his honour. *P. dayanum* is one of the most distinguished of these and Day flowered it in 1860 from an importation by Messrs. Low & Co. of Clapton. It was, in fact, Sir Hugh Low who had discovered it on Mount Kinabalu in northern Borneo in 1856.

Paphiopedilum dayanum is a most distinctive orchid, readily recognised by its large flowers characterised by a narrow but long dorsal sepal, oblanceolate unspotted petals with long ciliate fringes, and a transversely reniform staminode with obscure apical teeth. The petals rarely have some fine spotting along the upper margin in the basal half. Its leaves are amongst the most boldly tessellated in the genus and can have either a

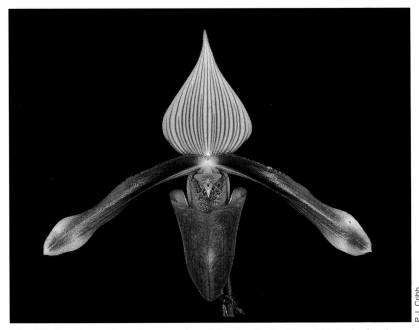

P.J. Cribb

Fig. 73. *Paphiopedilum dayanum*, in cultivation in the Royal Botanic Gardens, Kew.

A. Lamb

Fig. 74. *Paphiopedilum dayanum* growing in its natural habitat at Penibukan Ridge, Kinabalu.

Fig. 75. Close-up of a flower of *Paphiopedilum dayanum.*

Fig. 76. Close-up of a flower of *Paphiopedilum dayanum* from the slopes of Kinabalu.

bluish green (glaucous) or yellow-green hue. Fowlie (1984) has suggested that *Cypripedium burbidgei* of Reichenbach is the bluish-green-leaved variant of *P. dayanum* while the form with yellow-green leaves corresponds to Reichenbach's *Cypripedium petri*. The types of both were discovered by F.W. Burbidge (Fig. 11) and Peter Veitch on Mount Kinabalu in 1877. Whilst agreeing that *C. petri* should be considered synonymous with *P. dayanum*, I cannot support his view of *C. burbidgei*. Examination of the type specimens suggests that Rolfe (1896) was correct in suggesting the latter to be a hybrid of *P. dayanum* and *P. virens* (*P. javanicum* var. *virens*). The two preserved flowers in the Reichenbach herbarium are intermediate in sepal and petal shape and petal spotting and ciliation between the postulated parents. The plant figured by Fowlie (1984) as *P. burbidgei* is, in my opinion, quite typical of *P. dayanum*.

Paphiopedilum dayanum has only ever been collected on the lower slopes of Mount Kinabalu where it grows in leaf litter under bamboo and at the base of trees on steep ridges that flank the mountains. Plants with glaucous and yellow-green leaves grow here intermingled. Fowlie (1984) gave a graphic description of its habitat where the orchid grows on serpentine outcrops under the shade of 6–10 m tall trees. Burbidge (1880) described their discovery of *C. petri* thus: "Now came a climb up a rocky pathway, besides which we noticed fine plants of *Cypripedium petreanum* [*sic*]". The type locality is now almost stripped of plants and, on a visit there in 1983, I saw fewer than 20 scattered over an area of a few hundred square metres.

Paphiopedilum dayanum (Lindl.) Stein, *Orchideenbuch* 464 (1892). Type: Borneo, cult. Hort. Soc. (holotype K!).
Cypripedium spectabile Rchb.f. (sphalm. for *superbiens*) var. *dayanum* Lindl. in *Gard. Chron.* 1860: 693 (1860).
C. superbiens Rchb.f. var. *dayanum* (Lindl.) Reichb.f., *Xenia Orchid.* 2: 10 (1860).
C. dayanum (Lindl.) Rchb.f. in *Bot. Zeit.* 20: 214 (1862).
C. ernestianum Hort. in *Journ. Hort.* 1887: 375, fig. 67 (1887). Type: not located.
C. petri Rchb.f. in *Gard. Chron.* n.s. 13: 680 (1880). Type: Kinabalu, hort. *Veitch* (holotype W!).
Paphiopedilum dayanum (Lindl.) Stein var. *petri* (Reichb.f.) Pfitzer in Engler, *Pflanzenr. Orch. Pleon.* 86 (1903).

Cordula dayana (Lindl.) Rolfe in *Orchid Rev.* 20: 2 (1912).
Paphiopedilum petri (Rchb.f.) Rolfe in *Orchid Rev.* 20: 2 (1912).

DESCRIPTION. A *terrestrial herb* with one to several clustered growths. *Leaves* 4–6, oblong-lanceolate, obtuse and minutely bidenticulate at apex, up to 21 cm long, 5 cm wide, margins towards apex minutely serrate, tessellated dark and light yellow- or bluish-green. Inflorescence 1-flowered; peduncle up to 25 cm long, maroon, densely purple-pubescent; bract lanceolate, acute, up to 2.5 cm long, pale green, pubescent. *Flowers* up to 14.5 cm across, sepals white veined green, petals purplish, lip deep maroon and staminode green with darker veins; ovary up to 7 cm long, dull green, pubescent. *Dorsal sepal* ovate, acuminate, 5–6 cm long, 3-3.8 cm wide, ciliate. *Synsepal* ovate, acute, up to 5 cm long, 2 cm wide. *Petals* oblanceolate-spathulate, obtuse to acute, 7–8.5 × 1.5–1.8 cm, purple-ciliate. *Lip* 5–6.6 cm long, 2–2.9 cm wide, with a ciliate apical margin; side-lobes incurved, warted. *Staminode* transversely elliptic-reniform, shortly apiculate, 6 mm long, 13 mm wide. 2n = 34, 36.

DISTRIBUTION. Borneo, Sabah only; 300–1450 m altitude.

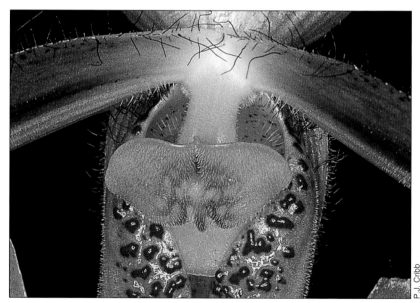

Fig. 77. Detail of the staminode of *Paphiopedilum dayanum*.

14. PAPHIOPEDILUM JAVANICUM var. VIRENS

T he original collections of this orchid were made on Mount Kinabalu by Hugh Low. The type plant came from his collection and was flowered by John Day of Tottenham in 1863. It was described as *Cypripedium virens* by H.G. Reichenbach in the same year. John Day's watercolour of the orchid survives at Kew.

R.S. Beaman

Fig. 78. Close-up of a flower of *Paphiopedilum javanicum* var. *virens* from Sabah.

Its affinity with *P. javanicum* was recognised by both Veitch (1889) and Stein (1892), both of whom relegated it to varietal rank. It differs from typical *P. javanicum* in having a greener flower and more nearly horizontal shorter petals. The variability of the Javanese and Balinese populations of *P. javanicum* that I have seen is considerable and plants which closely approach the Bornean specimens in petal attitude and markings are not infrequent. I have not seen living Sumatran or Flores plants of *P. javanicum* but the herbarium material seen confirms that *virens* falls within the overall range of variability of *P. javanicum*.

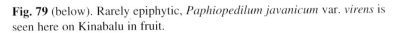

Fig. 79 (below). Rarely epiphytic, *Paphiopedilum javanicum* var. *virens* is seen here on Kinabalu in fruit.

A. Lamb

Fig. 80 (above). *Paphiopedilum javanicum* var. *virens* growing in its natural habitat on Kinabalu.

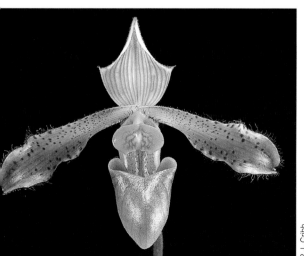

Fig. 81 (left). *Paphiopedilum javanicum* var. *virens* in cultivation at the Royal Botanic Gardens, Kew.

P.J. Cribb

Fowlie (1974b), in describing *P. purpurascens*, compared it with *P. virens* but not *P. javanicum*. It is as close to many of the wild and cultivated variants of *P. javanicum* that I have seen as it is to var. *virens*. The illustration of *P. javanicum* from Gunung Argowayang often used in *Orchid Digest* (e.g. 44: 99 & 45: 87) is not at all typical of the species. Most Javanese plants have less heavily spotted and less strongly deflexed petals, a staminode with more pronounced lateral teeth at the apex and an ovate dorsal sepal.

The type of *P. purpurascens* was a single plant collected by Mrs Sheila Collenette on Mount Kinabalu from a colony of typical var. *virens*. I have no hesitation therefore in reducing it to the synonymy of that variety.

Var. *virens* is found only on the lower slopes on Mount Kinabalu , in the adjacent Crocker Range in Sabah, and in the Kelabit Highlands of Sarawak. One of its major populations has recently been exterminated in an area of forest on the Pinosok Plateau destroyed to make way for a golf course. Elsewhere, even within the Kinabalu Park, it has suffered the depredations of collectors.

Its usual habitat in Sabah is in deep shade on steep, boulder strewn slopes often above rivers and streams in primary montane forest at elevations of 900–1650 m. It grows in leaf litter often in the cracks between boulders in deep shade.

The typical variety of *P. javanicum* is a widespread plant, one of the most widely distributed of all the slipper orchids in the Malay Archipelago. John Lindley (1821) first mentioned this species following his description of *P. insigne* in *Collectanea Botanica*, when he referred to plants similar to the latter which had been collected in Java by Dr Horsfield. Lindley eventually described it as *Cypripedium javanicum* in 1850 based on a collection and watercolour illustration by Reinwardt, who gave the species its name.

Paphiopedilum javanicum var. *javanicum* is widespread in Java where it has been subjected to heavy pressure from plant collectors. In Bali, it may already have been exterminated in the wild by collectors (J.B. Comber, pers. comm.) whilst in Sumatra, it has only been seen infrequently and is apparently a naturally rare species.

In Java, it grows as a terrestrial in montane forest at elevations between 950 and 2000 m but commonly at 1400–1700 m. It prefers partial to deep shade growing in leaf litter often amongst boulders on the forest floor. The soils in much of Java are volcanic and Fowlie (1980b) reports it growing in a mixture of black volcanic soil and humus at *c*. 1700 m in east Java. I have seen colonies in both east and west Java growing in montane forest on the slopes of volcanoes. The colonies were usually small and of about 100 plants or less growing on steep slopes in the forest in leaf litter and amongst boulders.

Pfitzer (1903) recognised as var. *minor* a Sumatran plant flowered in the Berlin Botanic Gardens. Small flowers are often produced by plants in

C.L. Chan

Fig. 82 (above). A rare occurence of a two-flowered inflorescence of *Paphiopedilum javanicum* var. *virens*.

cultivation. A plant of var. *virens* flowering at Kew in spring 1985 likewise had a very small flower on one growth but a normal flower on another of the same collection.

Several collections for the island of Flores, east of Java, have been tentatively ascribed to *P. javanicum* by J.J. Smith in his unpublished notes, now kept at Leiden. Examination of the specimens and Smith's sketches of the flower of a collection (*Posthumus* 3348) lead me to the same conclusion. The sepal and staminode shapes are well preserved and agree with those of *P. javanicum* from Java and Bali. The petals are possibly less heavily spotted along their length but otherwise also agree well.

Paphiopedilum javanicum is allied to *P. dayanum* It differs however in having smaller differently coloured flowers, a reniform staminode with projecting lateral teeth at the apex, a shorter less acuminate dorsal sepal and shorter spotted petals with only shortly ciliate margins. Var. *virens* probably occasionally hybridises with *P. dayanum* in the wild in northern Borneo. The resulting hybrid has been called *P. burbidgei*, having been first collected by Burbidge and Peter Veitch on Mount Kinabalu.

Paphiopedilum javanicum (Reinw. ex Lindl.) Pfitzer in *Pringsh. Jahrb. Wiss. Bot.* 19: 165 (1888), in Engler, *Bot. Jahrb.* 19: 49 (1894) & in Engler, *Pflanzenr. Orch. Pleon.* 85 (1903); Fowlie in *Orchid Dig.* 44: 97 (1980). Type: copy of Reinwardt illn. in Lindley herbarium at Kew.
Cypripedium javanicum Reinw. ex Lindl. in Paxton's *Fl. Gard.* 1: 38 (1850).

var. **virens** (Rchb.f.) Stein, *Orchideenbuch* 471 (1892).
Cypripedium virens Rchb.f. in *Bot. Zeit.* 21: 128 (1863). Type: Borneo, cult. *Day* (holotype W!).
C. javanicum Reinw. ex Lindl. var. *virens* (Rchb.f.) Veitch, *Man.* 4: 35 (1881).
Paphiopedilum virens (Rchb.f.) Pfitzer in Engler, *Bot. Jahrb.* 19: 41 (1896) & in Engler, *Pflanzenr. Orch. Pleon.* 84 (1903).
P. purpurascens Fowlie in *Orchid Dig.* 38: 155 (1974). Type: cult. Los Angeles Arb., *Hilberg* H 66 B1 (holotype UCLA!) **synon. nov.**

DESCRIPTION. A *terrestrial herb. Leaves* spreading, 4–5, narrowly elliptic, obtuse at minutely tridenticulate apex, 12–23 cm long, 3.4–4 cm wide, pale green, veined and lightly mottled darker green. *Inflorescence* 1-flowered; peduncle 16–36 cm long, purple, shortly white-pubescent; bract elliptic, obtuse, 1.5–2.5 cm long, 1–1.4 cm wide, ciliate on margins and mid-vein, pale green, very lightly spotted with purple. *Flower* 8–9.5 cm across; dorsal sepal pale green with darker green veins and a whitish pink margin; synsepal pale green; petals pale green with a pink-purple apical third, finely spotted with dark maroon in basal half to three-quarters; lip bright green with darker veins; pedicel and ovary 4.3–5 cm long, rather sparsely pubescent on ridges. *Dorsal sepal* ovate to elliptic, acuminate, 3–3.8 cm long, 2.5–2.9 cm wide, shortly ciliate, pubescent on outer surface. *Synsepal* lanceolate, acute, 2.5–2.6 cm long, 1.1–1.3 cm wide, pubescent on outer surface. *Petals* usually deflexed slightly from the horizontal, spatulate, obtuse, 4.2–4.8 cm long, 1.3–1.4 cm wide, shortly ciliate. *Lip* 3.6–4 cm long, 1.8–2 cm wide, very shortly pubescent on outer surface, verrucose on side-lobes. *Staminode* convex, reniform, 8 mm long, 10 mm wide, shortly pubescent all over surface. 2n = 36, 38.

DISTRIBUTION. North-east Borneo: Sabah and Sarawak; 900–1650 m altitude.

Are there more Slipper orchids to be found in Borneo?

S lipper orchids are showy plants and it would be logical to suppose that the Bornean ones are well-known and that no more await discovery. However, two factors suggest that more may be found in the future. The first flush of discovery in Borneo occurred in the second half of the last century through the activities of plant hunters and explorers, notably Hugh Low, Thomas Lobb and Frederick Burbidge. Of the currently known taxa, more than half were discovered during this period. Nearly all of these were collected in areas either close to the coast or accessible from one of the major rivers that penetrate the north coast of the island.

Little more was found until recently. Two World Wars undoubtedly distracted attention from Borneo and its plant wealth but it is still strange that no novelties appeared. I believe that this was, in part, due to the lack of specialist interest in the island's plants, but also because of the relative inaccessibility of the island's interior.

Air travel has undoubtedly made travel to Borneo and travel within the island easier. Furthermore remote tracts of country are now accessible by logging roads and tracks. In many ways the last wild places on the island are now being explored. This has led to some remarkable discoveries in recent years. *Paphiopedilum supardii* was discovered in the 1930s but not recognised as a new species until fifty years later. It was rediscovered by de Vogel in 1974 and again in the 1980s by the commercial collector after whom it was named. *P. kolopakingii* is a remarkable orchid, even in a genus of note such as *Paphiopedilum*. It is a large plant with a long, multi-flowered inflorescence, unlikely to have been overlooked by previous explorers if they had chanced upon it. Finally *P. philippinense*, an orchid that is widespread in the Philippines, was collected on an island off the east coast of Sabah in 1982 and in 1996 on the mainland in Sabah.

If the number of recorded species of *Paphiopedilum* is recorded against the surface area in square kilometres of all countries in Southeast Asia and the western Malay Archipelago where they occur. This shows that slipper orchids are over-represented in Sabah and Sarawak but under-represented in Kalimantan. This suggests that more slipper orchids remain to be discovered in Kalimantan. However, it is likely that the comparative wealth of Sabah and Sarawak is a reflection of their diverse topography, geology, soils and forest types. Suitable habitat is not as widespread in Kalimantan where much of the country is low altitude swamp forest, limestone is restricted and ultrabasic rocks very rare. Nevertheless it is true that Kalimantan is very poorly collected compared with Sabah, Sarawak and Brunei and, if new species are to be discovered, they are most likely to be found in its mountainous interior.

Bibliography and Further Reading

Albert, V.A. (1994). Cladistic relationships of the slipper orchids (Cypripedioideae: Orchidaceae) from congruent morphological and molecular data. *Lindleyana* 9: 115–132.

Albert, V.A. & M.A. Chase (1992). *Mexipedium*: a new genus of slipper orchid (Cypripedioideae: Orchidaceae) *Lindleyana* 7: 172–176.

Alexander, C. (1984). *Paphiopedilum sanderianum. Kew Mag.* 1: 3, t. 1.

Asher, J. (1980–1). A checklist for the genus *Paphiopedilum* for 1980–81. *Orchid Dig.* 44: 175–185; 213–228 45: 15–26; 57–64.

—— (1983). *Paphiopedilum adductum* Asher, new species from the Philippines, with notes about *P. rothschildianum* (Rchb.f.) Pfitzer and *P. elliottianum* (O'Brien) Fowlie. *Orchid Dig.* 47: 213–236.

Atwood, J.T. (1984). The relationships of the slipper orchids (subfamily *Cypripediodeae*), Orchidaceae. *Selbyana* 7: 129–247.

—— (1985). Pollination of *Paphiopedilum rothschildianum*: brood-site deception. *National Geogr. Research,* Spring 1985 247–254.

Atwood, J.T. & Williams, N.H. (1978). The utility of epidermal cell features in *Phragmipedium* and *Paphiopedilum* (Orchidaceae) for determining sterile specimens. *Selbyana* 2: 356–366.

—— (1979). Surface features of the adaxial epidermis in the conduplicate-leaved *Cypripedioideae* (Orchidaceae. *J. Linn. Soc. Bot.* 78: 141–156.

Bänziger, H. (1996). The mesmerizing wart: the pollination stategy of epiphytic lady slipper orchid *Paphiopedilum villosum* (Lindl.) Stein. *J. Linn. Soc. Bot.* 121: 59–90.

Birk, L. (1983). *The Paphiopedilum Grower's Manual*. L. Birk, Santa Barbara, California, U.S.A.

Blume, C.L. (1858). *Flora Javae* 139–143. Amsterdam, Netherlands.

Braem, G. (1988). *Paphiopedilum.* BrückeVerlag Kurt Schmersow, D–3200 Hildesheim, Germany.

Braem, G. & Loeb, U.W. (1985). *Paphiopedilum supardii* Braem & Loeb, spec. nov. *Die Orchidee* 36: 142–143.

Brieger, F.G. (1973). 3. *Paphiopedilum*, in Schlechter, R., *Die Orchideen* (ed. 3) 171–185. Paul Parey, Berlin.

Burbidge, F. (1880). *The Gardens in the Sun.* J. Murray, London.

Cribb, P.J. (1983). A synopsis of the genus *Paphiopedilum. The Plantsman* 4: 193–212.

Cribb, P.J. (1987). *The genus Paphiopedilum.* Collingridge, London.

Cribb, P.J., Campbell, J. & Dennis, G. (1985). *Paphiopedilum* in the Solomon Islands – the rediscovery of *P. "dennisii". Orchid Rev.* 93: 130–131.

Darwin, C. (1862*). On the various contrivances by which British and foreign orchids are fertilised.* J. Murray, London, U.K.

Delpino, F. (1873). Ulteriori Osservasione etc. *Atti Soc. Ital. Sci.* 16: 200.

Dodson, C.L. & van der Pijil, L. (1966). *Orchid flowers. Their pollination and evolution.* Univ. of Miami Press, U.S.A.

Dressler, R. (1981). *The Orchids. Natural History and Classification.* Harvard Univ. Press, Cambridge, Mass., U.S.A.

Duncan, R.E. (1959). List of chromosome numbers in orchids, in Withner, C. (ed.) *The Orchids: a scientific survey*: 529–587. Ronald Press Co., New York, U.S.A.

Duncan, R.E. & Macleod, R.A. (1949b). The chromosomes of some of the *Polyantha. Idem* 18: 159–163.

Fowlie, J.A. (1966). An annotated checklist of the species of *Paphiopedilum*, 1966. *Orchid Dig.* 30: 307–313.

—— (1974b). A clarification of *Paphiopedilum virens* (Rchb.f.) Pfitz., including a description of a new species, *Paphiopedilum purpurascens*. *Idem* 38: 153–157.

—— (1974c). *Paphiopedilum robinsonii* (Ridley.) Ridley. *Idem* 38: 163.

—— (1980a). *Paphiopedilum elliottianum* refound in the Philippines with some thoughts on the distribution of members of the section *Coryopedilum*. *Idem* 44: 70.

—— (1980b). Malaya revisited: part 16. *Idem* 44: 97–101.

—— (1981). Malaya revisited: part 19. *Idem* 45 165–169.

—— (1984). Malaya revisited: part 26. *Idem* 48: 169–174.

Garay, L.A. (1997). *Paphiopedilum lynniae*. *Lindleyana* 12: 233.

Gruss, O. (1997). *Paphiopedilum lowii* (Lindley) Stein. *Die Orchidee* 48: Orchideenkartei Seite 3, 847–848.

Hallier, H. (1896). Ueber *Paphiopedilum amabile* .... *Ann. Jard. Bot. Buitenzorg* 14: 18–52.

Karasawa, K. (1979). Karyomorphological studies in *Paphiopedilum*, Orchidaceae. *Bull. Hiroshima Bot. Gard.* 2: 1–149.

—— (1982a). Karyomorphological studies on four species of *Paphiopedilum*. *Idem* 5: 70–79.

—— (1982b). *The genus Paphiopedilum*. Karasawa, Hiroshima, Japan.

Karasawa, K. & Saito, K. (1982). A revision of the genus *Paphiopedilum* (Orchidaceae). *Bull. Hiroshima Bot. Gard.* 5: 1–69.

Koopowitz, H. (1995). An annotated checklist of the genus *Paphiopedilum*. *Orchid Digest* 59: 115–139.

Kraenzlin, F. (1897). *Orchidacearum Genera et Species.* Mayer & Mueller, Berlin.

Kramer, R. (1990). The unique pollination mechanisms of *Paphiopedilum sanderianum* (Rchb.f.) Stein. *Orchid Dig.* 54: 115–116.

Lindley, J. (1821). *Cypripedium insigne. Collectanea Bot.* t. 32. London, U.K.

Nilsson, L.A. (1979). Anthecological studies on the lady's slipper, *Cypripedium calceolus. Bot. Notis.* 132: 329–349.

Pfitzer, E.H. (1886). *Morphologische Studien ueber die Orchideenblüthe.* C. Winter, Heidelberg, W. Germany.

—— (1894). Beitrage zur Systematik der Orchideen. *Engler, Bot. Jahrb.* 19: 1–42.

—— (1903). Orchidaceae – Pleonandrae. I, in Engler, *Das Pflanzenreich* IV, 50 1–132.

Rafinesque, C.S. (1838). *Flora Telluriana* 4: 45–47. H. Pobasco, Philadelphia, U.S.A.

Rickett, H.W. & Stefleu, F.A. (1959). Nomina generica conservanda et rejicienda Spermatophytorum. *Paphiopedilum. Taxon* 8: 448–492.

Rolfe, R.A. (1986a). The *Cypripedium* group. *Orchid Rev.* 4: 327–334, 363–367.

—— (1896b). *Cypripedium nigritum. Idem* 4: 79–80.

Rosso, S.W. (1966). The vegetative anatomy of the *Cypripedioideae* (Orchidaceae). *J. Linn. Soc. Bot.* 59: 309–341.

Sander's *Complete List of Orchid Hybrids* (1947) & *Addenda* (1946–1960; 1961–1970; 1971–1975; 1976–1980, 1981–1985, 1986–1990, 1991–1995). St. Albans & London, U.K. & R.H.S., London

Schaffer, N. (1974). *Paphiopedilum sanderianum*: an enigma. *Orchid Dig.* 38: 233–236.

Schlechter, R. (1927). *Die Orchideen*, ed. 2. Paul Parey, Berlin.

Schoser, G. (1967b). *Paphiopedilum nigritum* (Rchb.f.) Pfitz. *Die Orchidee* 18: 117–121.

—— (1971). Species of the genus *Paphiopedilum*. *Proc. Sixth World Orchid Conf.* 111–114. Sydney, Australia.

Stein, B. (1892). *Orchideenbuch*. Paul Parey, Berlin.

Troll, W. (1951). Botanische Notizen II. *Abh. Math.-Nat.-Kl. Akad. Wiss. Mainz* 1951 (2).

Veitch, J. 91889). *Manual of Orchidaceous Plants* IV. *Cypripedium*. Veitch & Sons, Chelsea, U.K.

Valmayor, H. (1984). *Orchidiana Philippiniana*. E. Lopez, Manila, Philippines.

Veitch, J. (1889). *Manual of orchidaceous plants* IV. *Cypripedium*. Chelsea, U.K.

Vogel, S. (1962). Duftdrusen im Dienste der Bestaubung. *Abh. Math.-Natur. Kl. Akad. Mainz* 10: 601–763.

Warner R. (1878). *Cypripedium stonei platytaenium*. *Select Orchidaceous Plants* 3: t.14. Lovell Reeve & Co., London.

Webster, A.D. (1886). On the growth and fertilisation of *Cypripedium calceolus*. *Trans. Proc. Bot. Soc. Edinb.* 16: 337–360.

Williams, H. (1897). *Cypripedium stonei platytaenium*. In Warner, R. & H. Williams eds, *The Orchid Album* 11: t 496. B.S. Williams, London.

Wood, J.J. & P.J.Cribb (1994) *A Checklist of the Orchids of Borneo*. R.B.G. Kew.

Wood, M.W. (1976). Two recently introduced Philippine Paphiopedila. *Idem* 84: 350–353.

Yap, K.F. & Lee, T.M. (1972). *Paphiopedilum johorensis* Fowl. & K.F. Yap, *sp. nov.*, the Lady Slipper Orchid from Gunong Panti, Malaya. *Orchid Dig.* 36: 71–74.

Ziegenspeck, H. (1928). *Orchidaceae*, in Kirchner, E.O.O. *et al.*, *Lebensgeschichte der Bluetenpflanzen Mitteleuropas*. Stuttgart, W. Germany.

Acknowledgements

I would like to thank my colleagues Jim Comber, Jeffrey Wood and Sarah Thomas; Tony and Anthea Lamb, Simon Blakey, Chris Bailes, the late Dr Jack Fowlie, the late Rena George, Dr Ernst Grell, Dr Ed de Vogel, and Dr Suhirman, Sujiarti, Entim and Supardi of Kebun Raya, Bogor, Indonesia. I would also like to thank curators of the herbaria of the Forest Department, Sarawak, the Forest Herbarium, Sandakan, Sabah, Herbarium Bogoriense, Kew, Leiden, the Natural History Museum, London, Harvard University Herbaria, Paris, Singapore and Vienna for allowing me access to their collections. I would particularly like to thank Professor Gren Lucas, latterly Keeper of the Herbarium at Kew and his successor Professor Simon Owens for permission to use Kew's facilities in the preparation of this account.

George Argent, the late James Asher, Todd J. Barkman, Reed S. Beaman, C.L. Chan, Jim Comber, John Dransfield, Ernst Grell, P. Hans Hazebroek, Tony Lamb, S.P. Lim, W.M. Poon, K.M. Wong, and Yii Puan Ching have allowed me to use their photographs.

The inspiration for this book came from Chan Chew Lun and I am most grateful for his patience and enthusiasm in its preparation and publication.

114

Index

A

Anther 7

B

Boxall, William Fig. 14
Bullen, Mr 75
Burbidge, Frederick 9, 87, 89, Fig. 11

C

CITES 25
classification 27
column 7, Fig. 7
conservation 25
Cordula dayana 98
C. lawrenceana 93
C. lowii 73
C. rothschildiana 64
C. stonei 55
Crocker Range 102
Cypripedium 22, 27
C. amabile 78
C. burbidgei 97
C. calceolus 21
C. cannartianum 36
C. elliottianum 64
C. ernestianum 97
C. hookerae 82
C. hookerae var. *amabile* 78
C. hookerae var. *bullenianum* 78
C. hookerae var. *volonteanum* 82, 86
C. javanicum 104
C. laevigatum 36

C. lawrenceanum 93
C. lowii 73
C. neoguineense 56
C. petri 97
C. robinsonii 75, 78
C. roebelenii 31
C. rothschildianum 64
C. sanderianum 42
C. spectabile var. *dayanum* 97
C. stonei 55
C. virens 99, 104

D

Darwin, Charles 21
Day, John 49, 54, 94, Fig. 14
De Vogel, Eduard 13, 66, Fig. 15
Dideopsis aegrota 22, 64

E

Ecology 6, 15
Ericsson 10

F

Fitch, Walter 37
flower 6
flower, longitudinal section Fig. 6
flowering 19
Foerstermann 37

H

Handoyo, Hali 81
history 9
Hooker, Lady 81

I

Inflorescence 5
introduction 1

K

Klamm Mts 75
Kolopaking, Mr 45
Kinabalu, Mount 56, 68, 86, 102, Fig. 3

L

Lawrence, Sir Trevor 54
Liem Khe Wie 45, 67
life history 19
Linden, Jean 10, 56
Lindley, John 9, 68, Fig. 9
lip 7
Lohan River Fig. 16
Low, Hugh 9, 68, 81, 82, 94
Low, Messrs. 9, 68, 75, 81, 82, 94

M

Meratus Mountains 13
Mexipedium 27
Mulu, Gunong 10

N

New Bulb Co. 91
Nielsen, Ivan 37

O

Ovary 6, Fig. 8

P

Paphiopedilum adductum 59, 65
P. amabile 74, 75, 78

P. appletonianum 77
P. barbatum 90
P. bougainvilleanum 77
P. bullenianum var. **bullenianum** 9, 15, 18, 28, 30, 74–80, Figs 59–61
P. bullenianum var. *celebesense* 78
P. burbidgei 104
P. callosum 90
P. celebesense 74, 78
P. 'ceramensis' 78
P. dayanum 9, 15, 18, 25, 26, 28, 29, 75, 94–98, 104, Figs 1, 73–77
P. delenatii 27
P. druryi 77
P. elliottianum 59, 64
P. glanduliferum 59, 66
P. haynaldianum 72
P. hennisianum 22, 90
P. hookerae var. **hookerae** 9, 13, 15, 28, 30, 75, 77, 78, 81–82, Fig. 62
P. hookerae var. **volonteanum** 22, 30, 82–86, Figs 63–66
P. insigne 22, 75, 102
P. javanicum var. *javanicum* 99, 102, 103
P. javanicum var. **virens** 9, 15, 18, 22, 26, 28, 30, 97, 99–105, Figs 78–82
P. Jogjae 55
P. johorense 74, 77, 78
P. kolopakingii 14, 25, 29, 45–48, 106, Figs 33–35
P. laevigatum 36
P. lawrenceanum 10, 13, 15, 28, 30, 87–93, Figs 67, 71

P. lawrenceanum 'Hockbridgense'
Fig. 72
P. lawrenceanum var. *hyeanum*
93, Fig. 70
P. lawrenceanum var. *trieuanum*
Fig. 69
P. lawrenceanum var. *viride*   Fig.
68
P. linii   74, 75, 78
P. lowii var. **lowii**   9, 15, 18, 28,
68–73, Figs 54–57
P. lowii f. *aureum*   73, Fig. 58
P. lowii var. *aureum*   73
P. lowii var. *lynniae*   74
P. lowii var. *richardianum*   73
P. mastersianum   75
P. Maudiae   10
P. micranthum   27
P. nigritum   91, 92
P. philippinense   14, 15, 18, 29,
31–36, 106, Figs 21–24,
Frontispiece
P. philippinense var. *cannartianum*
36
P. philippinense var. *roebelenii*
32
P. praestans   66
P. purpurascens   102, 104
P. purpuratum   22
P. randsii   32
P. richardianum   71
P. robinsonii   74, 78
P. roebelenii   31
P. rothschildianum   9, 13, 14, 15,
18, 22, 25, 26, 29, 56–64, 65,
Figs 19, 44–51
P. rothschildianum var.
elliottianum   64

P. sanderianum   10, 13, 14, 15,
18, 22, 24, 25, 29, 32, 37–44,
Figs 25–32
P. sect. Barbata   28
P. sect. Coryopedilum   28, 31, 37
P. sect. Pardalopetalum   28
P. stonei   15, 18, 25, 29, 49–55,
Figs 36–38, 40–43
P. stonei var. *candidum*   55
P. stonei var. *latifolium*   55
P. stonei var. *platytaenium*   51,
Fig. 39
P. stonei var. *stictopetalum*   55
P. subgenus Parvisepalum   27
P. supardii   13 14, 15, 25, 29, 59,
65–67, 106, Figs 52–53
P. topperi   47
P. tortipetalum   74, 78
P. villosum   22, 24
P. virens   75, 97
P. volonteanum   86
peloton   19
petals   6
Phragmipedium   22, 24, 27
plant   5
pollination   21
protocorm   19

R

Ravensway   10
Reichenbach, Heinrich G.   56, 75,
87, 94, Fig. 12
references
Ridley, Henry   75

S

Sander, Frederick   10, 37, 56,
Fig.10

Sander, Messrs   56, 81
seed   19
Selenipedium   22, 27
Sheridan-Lea, Phyllis   75
Simanis Nursery   13, 45
staminode   Fig. 5, 7
Stone, Mr   49
Supardi   13

T
Topper, Richard   47

V
Veitch, Messrs. James   9, 81

W
Waterstradt   13
Whitehead, John   10

Y
Yii Puan Ching   73

Other titles available through *Natural History Publications:*

Mount Kinabalu: Borneo's Magic Moutain—an introduction to the natural history of one of the world's great natural monuments *by* K.M. Wong & C.L. Chan

Kinabalu: Summit of Borneo (*eds*. K.M. Wong & A. Phillipps)

Kinabalu: The Haunted Mountain of Borneo *by* C.M. Enriquez (Reprint)

A Colour Guide to Kinabalu Park *by* S.K. Jacobson

Parks of Sabah *by* A. Phillipps

The Larger Fungi of Borneo *by* D.N. Pegler

Pitcher-plants of Borneo *by* A. Phillipps & A. Lamb

Nepenthes of Borneo *by* C. Clarke

Rafflesia: Magnificent Flower of Sabah *by* Kamarudin Mat Salleh

Tree Flora of Sabah and Sarawak Vol. 1 (*eds*. E. Soepadmo & K.M. Wong)

Tree Flora of Sabah and Sarawak Vol. 2. (*eds*. E. Soepadmo, K.M. Wong & L.G. Saw)

Trees of Sabah Vol. 1 *by* P.F. Cockburn

Trees of Sabah Vol. 2 *by* P.F. Cockburn

Dipterocarps of Sabah *by* W. Meijer & J. Wood

The Morphology, Anatomy, Biology and Classification of Peninsular Malaysian Bamboos *by* K.M. Wong

The Bamboos of Peninsular Malaysia *by* K.M. Wong

The Bamboos of Sabah *by* S. Dransfield

Rattans of Sabah *by* J. Dransfield

The Plants of Mount Kinabalu 1: Ferns *by* B.S. Parris *et al.*

The Plants of Mount Kinabalu 2: Orchids *by* J.J. Wood *et al.*

Orchids of Borneo Vol.1 *by* C.L. Chan *et al.*

Orchids of Borneo Vol. 2 *by* J.J. Vermeulen

Orchids of Borneo Vol. 3 *by* J.J. Wood

A Checklist of the Orchids of Borneo *by* P.J. Cribb & J.J. Wood

Orchids of Java *by* J.B. Comber

Flowers and Plants of Mount Kinabalu *by* T. Sato

Mosses and Liverworts of Mount Kinabalu *by* Frahm *et al.*

Birds of Mount Kinabalu, Borneo *by* G.W.H. Davison

Proboscis Monkeys of Borneo *by* E.L. Bennett & F. Gombek

The Natural History of Orang-utan *by* E.L. Bennett

A Field Guide to the Mammals of Borneo *by* J. Payne *et al.*

Checklist of Lizards of Sabah *by* Tan Fui Lian
The Systematics and Zoogeography of the Amphibia of Borneo *by* R.F. Inger (Reprint)
The Natural History of Amphibians and Reptiles in Sabah *by* R.F. Inger & Tan Fui Lian
A Field Guide to the Frogs of Borneo *by* R.F. Inger & R.B. Stuebing
Pocket Guide to the Birds of Borneo *by* C.M. Francis
Birds of Pelong Rocks *by* M. Wong & Hj. Mohammad bin Hj. Ibrahim
The Fresh-water Fishes of North Borneo *by* R.F. Inger & P.K. Chin
Termites of Sabah *by* R.S. Thapa
Forest Pest Insects in Sabah *by* V.K. Chey
Common Seashore Life of Brunei *by* M. Wong & Aziah binte Hj. Ahmad
Common Lowland Rainforest Ants of Sabah *by* Arthur Chung
Borneo: the Stealer of Hearts *by* O. Cooke (Reprint)
Land Below the Wind *by* A. Keith (Reprint)
A Sabah Gazetteer *by* J. Tangah & K.M. Wong
In Brunei Forests: An Introduction to the Plant Life of Brunei Darussalam *by* K.M. Wong (Revised edition)
A Walk through the Lowland Rainforest of Sabah *by* E.J.F. Campbell
Manual latihan pemuliharaan dan penyelidikan hidupan liar di lapangan *by* A. Rabinowitz (*Translated by* Maryati Mohamad)
Enchanted Gardens of Kinabalu: A Borneo Diary *by* S.M. Phillipps
The Theory and Application of a Systems Approach to Silvicultural Decision-making *by* M. Kleine
Dipsim: A Dipterocarp Forest Growth Simulation Model for Sabah *by* R. Ong & M. Kleine
Kadazan Dusun–Malay–English Dictionary (*eds.* R. Lasimbang *et al.*)
An Introduction to the Traditional Costumes of Sabah (*eds.* R. Lasimbang & S. Moo-Tan)
Traditional Stone and Wood Monuments of Sabah *by* Peter R. Phelan